Psalms
for
Troubled
Times

Merrill Morse

NOVALIS / The Liturgical Press

Cover by David Manahan, O.S.B.

Novalis
P.O. Box 990, Outremont, P. Q. H2V 4S7 Canada

The Liturgical Press
Collegeville, Minnesota, United States of America, 56321

ISBN:
Novalis: 2-89088-497-X
The Liturgical Press: 0-8146-1968-1

1	2	3	4	5	6	7	8	9

Library of Congress Cataloging-in-Publication Data
Morse, Merril, 1948–
    Psalms for troubled times / Merrill Morse.
        p. cm.
        1. Bible. O.T. Psalms—Meditations. 2. Consolation. I. Title.
BS1430.4.M64 1991   90-29018
242'.5—dc20   CIP

Contents

Preface

Whenever brokenness enters our lives, we look for those resources that can guide and sustain us through our times of trial. For each of us the resources may vary. But for most of us they include the Scriptures, friends, and some kind of faith community in which we can struggle, pray, mourn, and seek comfort, company, and hope.

The essays that follow explore a variety of psalms as resources for the difficult days on our life journeys. For the most part, these are unusual psalms in that many of them are not included in the weekly readings we hear at church. That is because these psalms are often rather dark, angry, and intensely personal. They do not necessarily make for the most appropriate readings for worshiping communities on Sunday mornings.

But they have a value that these essays seek to uncover. In their own unique way these lament and imprecatory psalms, as they are called, can also be a resource for dealing with life's stresses and sorrows.

Along with Scripture, friends and supportive communities provide a great resource for survival and growth. Among such resources in this author's life are people who have mediated grace and provided support not only through life's struggles in general but particularly during the writing of this book. Thanks from the heart go to LeAnn, Deborah, Marilyn, Beulah, Greg, Lenny, Cathy, and a number of other good friends, including the members of the Bethel House Bible Study Group, where the gospel is more than a topic of study; it is a way people seek to live.

Also, I wish to thank the staff and editors of The Liturgical Press for their able assistance in this undertaking. Not only do they have a strong commitment to a valuable publications ministry; they are also cordial people with whom to work.

Finally, a note on the Scripture texts used is in order. The Revised Standard Version of the Bible serves as the basis for the psalms quoted here. However, some alterations have been made by the author toward more inclusive language. These will be noted with brackets.

References to God as male have been altered except where such alterations would create a very awkward text or one that would lose the important sense of intimacy conveyed by a personal pronoun. Similarly, most generic references to ''man'' and males have been altered, except where the sense of the text would be significantly affected, where the intensity of the text would be diminished, or where such changes would be of little relevance to the meaning of the text as a whole.

A completely inclusive version of the psalms in the same tone as the RSV text was not available at the time of this writing. Current inclusive-language Lectionary versions of the psalms do not include most of the passages quoted here. Comparisons were made, however, with *Inclusive-Language Psalms* (New York: The Pilgrim Press, 1987) and *Psalms Anew in Inclusive Language,* tr. Nancy Schreck and Maureen Leach (Winona, Minn.: St. Mary's Press, 1986). While the results may be imperfect, it is nevertheless hoped that a certain sensitivity will have been demonstrated in regard to this important issue.

Epiphany, 1991

Introduction

There are a lot of books around for people who are hurting or in trouble. But most of them deal with the kind of suffering that is caused by external events such as death, accidents, or disease. So what about the kind of trouble that we create for ourselves? How do we face the pain that comes from our own failures—from addictions, affairs, abuse, dependencies, divorce, or other forms of self-destructive behavior?

That is not to say that we are totally or solely to blame for the existence of such trials in our lives. Sometimes they have very complicated histories. But no matter where they come from or how they take shape in our lives, we know that we ourselves have had something to do with their existence. We ourselves are in some way accused.

When a drunken driver randomly smashes into our car, we can easily blame someone else for the tragedy. When death comes to a loved one, either through something like cancer or simply old age, we have an external, abstract reality to blame.

But with the kind of conflicts that arise from our own chemical dependencies or marital infidelity, for example, we know that we cannot finally blame the problems on some outside, impersonal reality. To do so would be self-deceptive. Somehow, whether we are the guilty party or closely connected to someone who is, we cannot help but feel blamed ourselves. There is usually a piece of us deep inside that feels painfully involved in the creation of such

7

situations. The accusing finger—our own, God's, or someone else's—seems to point at us.

In the times of our failures we often discover an inner darkness. We tremble before our own fears and shame. We wonder how to deal with the frightening possibilities that lie within us.

A host of questions floods our minds at such times. How will we survive? Will there ever be healing? Where can we find love and forgiveness again? These cries inside us need to be voiced lest we be consumed by our own distress.

Yet how can we process the guilt that we feel when our lives have gone off track? How can we express the sorrow or anger—or both—that surfaces when our lives have been broken by our own fallibility? Where can we go to find words of release, words to express our reality, words to give us both comfort and hope? How can we speak when we feel so profoundly accused, either by ourselves or by others?

This book is an attempt to provide channels for our cries. It links the reader with the cries of others by connecting our voices to the laments and outbursts of those before us who have also wrestled with personal failure and with life's general unfairness.

This is a book for those who have failed, for those feeling wounded by their own choices or those of people close to them. Indeed, some of life's most painful failures come from deliberate choices we have made when our intentions were good but the consequences or reactions of others have been brutal. At such times life can backfire on us like a badly tuned car.

In truth, failure is normal. We all fail sometimes in life. Failure is part of being human. But transcending failure is also part of being human, perhaps even the greater part. To transcend failure requires first of all accepting it, then processing it, venting our frustrations about it, and finally, looking beyond it to something new.

The meditations in this book are meant to be a step toward transcending the hurts and burdens caused by our failures. They can, hopefully, give greater shape to our sorrows, reminding us that we are not alone, either in our brokenness or in our desire for healing and restoration.

Texts of Transcendence

The texts that provide the basis for these meditations are chiefly the psalms of the Old Testament. These ancient words reflect a wide array of human experience. They speak of sorrow and joy, war and peace, cursing and blessing. They tell stories of human conflict and infidelity—between friend and friend, between husband and wife, between humanity and God. But they also speak of hope and restoration, of forgiveness and a second chance.

One of the amazing things about the psalms is how many of them are psalms of adversity. In their poetic way they preserve for us moving accounts of human anguish, of people struggling with suffering and seeking for truth. The individual stories behind these psalms are largely lost, but the message they maintain is eternal. Part of the reason they endure is that their story is so similar to ours. Indeed, that is why we can find in these old songs a channel for our own current cries.

Sometimes we may be surprised at the depth and passion of these passages. Their language is stronger, their images more vivid than we might choose for ourselves, even in cursing. These are not meek mumbles for some kind of divine deliverance. They are, rather, the anguished cries of the human spirit in times of great distress.

What makes these psalms so potent is that what they voice is so real. They do not shrink from the harsh realities of life. Love, grief, betrayal, fear of dying—these are just some of the critical life experiences to be found in the psalms. They are the enduring concerns of our lives, the deeper movements of the soul which weigh more heavily in our lives than superficial or material factors.

The psalms, of course, are also realistic about material life. They speak of our plainer daily needs as well as of our deeper spiritual ones. Yet whether they reflect our simple need for rest and food or the deeper moods of our soul, the psalms show us how common our struggles are—how ordinary and basic are all our needs. When personal suffering strips away what is superficial in life, then we see two things: (1) what it is to be human and (2) how we share these basic needs of *both* body and soul with those around us.

In many ways, of course, we live in a very different culture than that in which the psalms or other passages of Scripture were produced. We do not live in walled cities like those of ancient Israel, fearing attacks from neighboring tribes. Our civilization is much more sophisticated.

Or is it? In an era of corporate takeovers and competition at the office and in the marketplace, in an age where the world yet stands divided between opposing armies, we still know the tensions of personal, ethnic, and international conflict, just as did the authors of the psalms. In our lives, too, we experience treachery, divided families, gossiping neighbors, and adversaries. Our battlefields may be different from those of old, but the torments of our hearts have changed very little.

In many ways the elemental conflicts of life consume people today in much the same way as they did the authors of the psalms two to three thousand years ago. That tells us again that what the psalms portray is both powerful and real. It means we are never completely alone in our anguish. Instead, we are very deeply connected with the experiences of generations of people before us and with how they reacted to the trials and struggles of life. As they survived, so can we. From their experience, we can learn. Their words can become our own.

Struggle and Faith

There is another aspect of the psalms that we must consider in order to understand them correctly, which is that these psalms are all statements made in the context of faith in a living God. The psalmists did not cry into a vacuum. They believed that their words had meaning not only as a mechanism for venting their deepest emotions but also because they experienced this universe in which we live as fundamentally purposeful and benevolent. In their lives they held God accountable as One who understands and cares for our feelings and who has the capacity to renew and assist us.

One of the most striking lessons of the psalms is what they tell us about being free to lay before the Almighty every aspect of our lives—sorrows and failures included. All our experiences, all our fears, all our hopes and frustrations, even our bitterness and hostilities, may be laid in the lap of a loving God. There is nothing we experience which is beyond the knowledge or capacity of the divine to deal with. Whatever we bring is legitimate. It is God's job in the end to sift it, to distill for our lives that which is most valuable and redeeming.

In the meantime, the psalms give us trememdous permission to go somewhere in our lives with nothing hidden. That in itself is comfort. For in times of trial so much gets hidden in the wrestling of the soul. We need a place to let it all out, to be freed at least for a while from some of our burdens and fears, a place to confess and be heard. The psalms give us permission to do that.

In fact, they do more. They declare that the God who hears and cares and loves with an unending love is able to lift us up out of our darkness, to cleanse us within, and to create new possibilities for our lives. That is transcendence. That is our hope for going from being accused to being healed and free again. If the resources of Scripture can help us move in that direction, they are well worth pursuing.

How to Proceed

These are meditations for the accused, for those struggling with failure and pain. This book is divided into three sections dealing with the kind of issues and feelings we face when we are injured or accused.

First comes Words of Affliction—meditations on passages from the psalms that crystallize our anguish in times of intense suffering. Next comes Words of Adversity, which delve into the hostility we feel when confronted by interpersonal conflict and people whose actions hurt us. Third comes Words of Assurance, which help us to feel trust again and to sense the supportive intimacy that can help us to recover from times of struggle and failure. These are words of hope. They are a promise of new possibilities ahead, and they help renew our strength to pursue them.

Obviously, this book has an order. Our emotions, however, do not. Some days we need to go directly to words of comfort or hope. Other times we need to delve into the darker regions of our soul to crash around in our anger and pain much as a wounded animal might do. In a sense, that is what we are at such times. Sometimes we just need to cry—cries of anger, cries of sorrow, cries of pain.

Accordingly, it may be most helpful not to read these meditations straight through, but to pick and choose as suits the need. Taken together, they may provide spaces to go, and to go back to again and again, on our journey toward wholeness. If they do provide such space, or the comfort of linking our cries with the cries of others who have experienced failure and struggling before us, then they will have served their intended purpose.

Part I

Words of Affliction

1

Afflicted

Be gracious to me, O LORD, for I am languishing;
  O LORD, heal me, for my bones are troubled. . . .
I am weary with my moaning;
  every night I flood my bed with tears.

Psalm 6:2, 6a

For evils have encompassed me without number;
  my iniquities have overtaken me.

Psalm 40:12a

I am overcome by my trouble. . . .
  My heart is in anguish within me,   . . .
And I say, "O that I had wings like a dove!
  I would fly away and be at rest;. . .

Psalm 55:2, 4a, 6

Affliction comes. There are times in life when we are devastated, crushed by life's agonizing twists and turns. Sometimes we are the cause of our own undoing. Other times it is someone else who brings us down. Usually it is a combination of the two—our own personal failures and the misunderstandings, animosities, and disharmonies that arise when people of differing views come into conflict. However we are brought to the bottom, we never find it a welcome place to be. Sometimes it is so bad that we seek to drug ourselves, to lose ourselves in reckless behavior, even to contemplate suicide.

Affliction hurts, and its sting may not be redemptive. Granted, life holds a certain amount of pain for all of us, and struggle is a necessary part of growth. But there are some kinds of affliction that pass beyond the bounds of what is vital, helpful, or positive. Instead of growth marks, we are left with scars.

There are those who would console or rationalize with a fatalism that says, "It was meant to be." But there are some kinds of breakdowns in life that were simply not meant to be. Rather, they are a direct violation of what was meant to be, a tragic tear in the fabric of life. Even when the mending process produces a garment of more strength, the seam remains. There is a sorrow appropriate to the damage done.

It is important that we recognize these invasions of destruction into our lives and name them for what they are. For only by doing so can we properly mourn what has been injured or lost, those pieces of our lives that will never be the same again, no matter how much reconstructive surgery may follow. We must acknowledge the full pain of our wounds in order to prepare them for proper healing.

Healing, of course, takes time. Severe afflictions produce feelings of such intensity that it is not realistic to expect them to diminish too soon. Pain, anger, rage, grief, even a thirst for revenge—these are among the deepest and most powerful emotions we have.

Few people can comprehend the intensity of our emotions in our time of affliction. Those who only observe cannot hear the silent screams or agonized weeping within, cannot perceive the endless, all-pervasive heaviness of our spirit. They do not know how it intrudes into every aspect of daily life—reappearing suddenly around unexpected corners after an all-too-temporary respite. The weight of our affliction haunts our dreams and eats away at our self-confidence, our sanity, at the very life-force within us.

Affliction can be such a lonely experience. It is a valley through which each person must go alone. Sometimes we will be the only one who really knows what happened or why. No one else can step into our soul and feel exactly as we do. Who on the outside can ever fully understand the nuances of our devastation?

Judgment

Instead of understanding, affliction more often brings judgment. Indeed, being afflicted means having to live with the sentences pronounced by people who are distanced from the consequences we endure. Often we suffer the imposition of other people's values on our lives.

That is not to say that judgment is entirely out of line. In some circumstances the sentences of our peers are vital for the protection and improvement of the larger human community. But overall, judgment is almost always misplaced. It is as fallible as those who dispense it.

The human propensity to judge probably stems from the corrupted nature within us as it seeks to compensate for its own impotence, fear, and guilt by projecting them onto others. Judging is a way of hiding from ourselves and others the sins of our own commission.

Judgment will never be fair, for no human being can know the whole. It may be human nature to judge, but it is that same nature that corrupts all judgments we make. Only God can judge with accuracy and fairness. For humans to judge without sufficient recognition of the provisional nature of all judging is to usurp the role of God, to infringe upon that prerogative of divinity that is not rightly ours. Yet judgment inevitably becomes another burden added to affliction; it rubs salt into our already painful wounds.

No wonder, then, that affliction produces such anger. Anger is an essential outlet for the turmoil our hearts cannot contain; it is a vital part of the healing process. Sometimes the anger is misdirected, as we ourselves may recognize. Yet it provides a channel for venting the complex and restless energies that swirl around inside us.

We will need to let go of the anger eventually. When it has served its purpose it must be laid aside. Otherwise it can consume us as it distracts us from the healing we need. Often, that healing process is cyclical. Time and again we will need to return to our anger, to repeat the stages of shame, remorse, sorrow, and release until our energies are spent or sorted again into their proper places.

But the day will come when the affliction has passed. Our longing for escape will be fulfilled. We will find the wings to rise out of our oppression. We will be free of judgment and in need of the anger no more. Fortunately, life's afflictions are not eternal.

2

Trauma and Resistance

Save me O God!
  For the waters have come up to my neck.
I sink in deep mire,
  where there is no foothold;
I have come into deep waters,
  and the flood sweeps over me.
I am weary with my crying;
  my throat is parched. . . .
Insults have broken my heart,
  so that I am in despair.

Psalm 69:1-3a, 20a

First comes the trauma—the shock of being discovered. It feels like the ground is dissolving under your feet. Footholds give way, the water keeps rising, suffocation seems near.

Perhaps it begins when your spouse confronts you about the affair or the addiction. Maybe it comes with the notice about your job. It could be a church leader or supervisor appearing in your office or home to pronounce you suspended. It could even be a lawyer's letter or a policeman's voice informing you of the charges filed against you. It could simply be the explosion that hits a family when relationships are stretched past the breaking point. Inevitably, it involves coming face to face with an unpleasant reality, confronting a truth you would have preferred to avoid.

However it comes, it is horrible. Every cell of your body recoils in shock. You want to scream, "No, it's not true! Wait! I can explain. You don't understand." And maybe you're right. They *don't* understand. There is so much to explain. And some of the accusations may not be true at all.

But some of them are, and you know it. And your heart sinks in cold dread.

> Save me, O God!
>   For the waters have come up to my neck. . . .
> I have come into deep waters,
>   and the flood sweeps over me.
>
> Psalm 69:1, 2b

Sometimes the shock and the truth together overwhelm us. We let the waters rise and sweep over our heads. We give up our pretenses and defenses and let the tide wash us where it will. Sometimes it is even a relief to finally be free of the lies. Hiding can take such a toll. Whether we are keeping our own secrets or someone else's, the anxiety becomes too great a burden. We welcome the release of exposure.

Resistance

But sometimes we prefer to fight, thrashing against the currents that threaten to draw us under. Perhaps there is a piece of us that feels violated. It may be pride. It may be a reaction to broken trusts. It may even be honor—defending those truths that remain in the midst of the half-truths and untruths that have been spoken.

A lot of people don't understand the fighting response. They may write it off as denial, and sometimes they are right. But there is often more to it. For sometimes we fight to survive. When we feel attacked or threatened, it is only natural that our defense mechanisms kick in. In an intervention for someone who is chemically dependent, when an explosion comes in the family or at work, when we are arrested, suspended, or exposed, it takes strong psychological resistance just to deal with the trauma of the moment.

For surely we feel attacked. Even though we may know inside that the attack is justified in some way, our energies flow into the experience of the moment, reacting to the immediate threat.

That is not so hard to understand, and understanding it may help relieve some of the conflict when confrontations come. For this initial phase will pass.

There is a deeper dynamic to the fighting response that is longer term and more complex. The attack we experience is also the trigger to a new dimension of the battle within. There comes the moment when we recognize the stakes of the battle, when our very soul stands exposed to forces that could destroy us. Therein lies the true terror. Our resistance may manifest itself externally. Indeed, we may try to channel all our energy into the external battle to avoid the conflict within. But the deepest fear is of losing our soul, of our very self being consumed and destroyed.

To fight is to buy time both within and without. It is a way to preserve some control, to cling to a rock until the waters recede a little. To fight is not all bad. It can even be a way of holding on to one's sense of self-worth. The basis for that sense of self-worth may need to be revised later, but if one loses it altogether, the road back to healing can be even longer. At its best, the fighting response can remind us of the internal resources we have for facing the long journey ahead.

Danger

There are dangers in fighting. We can get so caught up in the fighting process that we never pass beyond it. We hide in the battle. Our relationships get polarized beyond healing.

Another danger is mistaking who our adversaries really are. If we blame the wrong persons as the source of our woes, we stand no chance of being healed. For when blame is misdirected, endless energy gets consumed in futile recriminations. False blaming is one of the greatest pitfalls of human conflict. It drains the spirit and directs everyone away from the root issues. In the end, there will be blame enough for all.

> I have come into deep waters. . . .
> Let not the flood sweep over me,
>   or the deep swallow me up,
>   or the pit close its mouth over me.
>
> Psalm 69:2b, 15

If the pit closes its mouth, there will be no new possibilities.

3

The Wasting Time

Be gracious to me, O LORD, for I am in distress;
    my eye is wasted from grief,
    my soul and my body also.
For my life is spent with sorrow,
    and my years with sighing;
my strength fails because of my misery,
    and my bones waste away.
I am the scorn of all my adversaries. . . .
    I have passed out of mind like one who is dead;
I have become like a broken vessel.

Psalm 31:9-10, 11a, 12

It gets in the bones—an ache so deep that the heart wants to break, a strange weakness penetrating both body and soul. Inner arms wrap around the pain, trying to hold together what is left. Sometimes all we can muster is a moan, a longing cry spilled out from the depths of our being in the hope that someone will hear—and care.

It is such a terrible thing to be so wounded, so decimated, so crushed. And it leaves one feeling so alone. To know such grief is to touch death. And to touch that inner death while the body still lives is an expensive experience. It spends the capital of the soul, which was meant to be invested in life. It is a costly enterprise indeed, this business of wasting away in body and soul.

Time stretches painfully, as the psalmist knew: "For my life is spent with sorrow." It seems that the grief will last forever, that it overwhelms all that has been, that it erases the good.

Such grief can push the sustaining memories of what was healthy deep into the mind, to places from which it is hard to recall them. Perhaps that is the mind's way of preserving and protecting what is good, lest the good be overwhelmed by the onslaught of destruction.

But the accompanying darkness and emptiness is a trial unto itself. Time stands still in this vacuum of despair. All the promises of a better future bounce with a hollow tone against the walls of gloom. Life itself seems tainted. Strength fails.

To add to the burden, there is the scorn that comes from others, the being forgotten, ignored, abandoned. Who will advocate for us in this realm of alienation? Few are willing to walk with us through the darkness. That there are any is reason for hope.

For one who has been active, socially engaged, or publicly acknowledged, there is a particular pain in "passing out of mind like one dead." It is a hard coming down. But if one finds solid ground at the bottom and a new perspective from which to see others and oneself with more honesty and compassion, then the coming down will have been useful.

On the way down, however, and for a while at the bottom, there is that broken-vessel sensation. To feel useless, like a shattered pot, is a miserable thing. Self-pity so easily floods in to fill the space created by the shattering. For one who has known usefulness and has valued self according to what one can accomplish, to be so undone is deeply humbling.

More than just the external forms are broken. The breaking is also of the soul. The old images and dreams lie in pieces, ready to be melted and remolded but with no guarantee of how they will be refashioned. Clearly, simply gluing will no longer suffice. One is past the point where the old glue holds.

It is a frightening prospect to face the furnace, this time in full consciousness of one's being. Those patterns that were familiar may have been extinguished forever. The phoenix-promises of the potter may speak of the essence being preserved in a new, more useful, and more beautiful vessel than before; but first one needs to mourn the familiar, the broken, the designs that were etched into one's clay over the years by the sharp edges of many cutters' tools.

In the meantime there is the gnawing plague of uselessness, of losing the value one felt through familiar functions. And there is the sad knowledge that when the new vessel is formed, it may not hold all that it contained before. The price of the new may be the exclusion of some of what was good about the old. It is a loss to be mourned.

Finally, there are those who would even rewrite our past, who change their perceptions and testimonies about what has been and what has not. And so we lose not only our present but also our past as we stand before an ambivalent future.

This is the place of wasting. Here is where the spirit languishes with that deep aching of both body and soul. Here our very bones seem to waste away—all those inner and outer support structures that once held us together. Now they creak and bend under the load and start to crumble. All we can do is cry.

> Take me out of the net which is hidden for me, . . .
> . . . set my feet in a broad place.
>
> Psalm 31:4a, 8b

4

Guilt

O LORD, rebuke me not in thy anger,
nor chasten me in thy wrath!
For thy arrows have sunk into me,
and thy hand has come down on me. . . .
There is no health in my bones
because of my sin.
For my iniquities have gone over my head;
they weigh like a burden too heavy for me. . . .
I am utterly bowed down and prostrate; . . .
For my loins are filled with burning,
and there is no soundness in my flesh.
I am utterly spent and crushed;
I groan because of the tumult of my heart. . . .
and the light of my eyes—it also has gone from me. . . .
But I am like a deaf man, I do not hear,
like a dumb man who does not open his mouth. . . .
For I am ready to fall,
and my pain is ever with me.

Psalm 38:1-2, 3b, 4, 6a, 7, 8, 10b, 13, 17

The guilt. What shall we do with the guilt? How can we stand to look into our soul and face the ugly signs of brokenness? How are we to bear having our failures exposed to others, being stripped naked in our guilt, made defenseless in our shame? Who does not wither before the unrelenting light of the clear and accusing truth?

We long to hide our shame, to cover our head, to run away from judgment. But there is nowhere that the searing light does not pierce. We are displayed. We are struck down. We are crushed by the weight of our own wrongdoing.

So real is its power that the pain within can even take physical form. Our bowels turn in turmoil; our hair grays; our joints ache. Diseases may even develop. In myriad ways the body reacts, displaying its inner wounds.

Guilt is such a heavy burden. It weighs us down like a slab of concrete pinning us to the ground. Each breath is a strain. The air of life comes laboriously into the lungs; even the will to breathe is constrained.

Guilt levels us, knocking us to our knees and sometimes further, until our faces press into the dust of our crumbled dreams. Guilt reduces us to a bended state where we clutch, head bowed, at the ache. Our tears fall in torrents, but they cannot wash away the stains we see inside. Rising from the hot pain of the soul, our salt-bitter tears seep out in painful cycles, only to disappear again into the parched wilderness our life has become.

> For thy arrows have sunk into me,
>   and thy hand has come down on me. . . .
> I am utterly spent and crushed;
>   I groan because of the tumult of my heart.
>
> Psalm 38:2, 8

Wounded. That is one of the feelings that accompanies guilt. The arrows that have sunk into us pierce tender places. They penetrate our core in ways that will take a long time to heal. We wonder if we will ever recover. Who can stop the bleeding, the slow draining of the soul? Will we ever be able to stand intact, to lead a normal life? If only we had made different choices!

This tumult of the heart is both tender and violent. We groan under self-accusations, the full force of our own failure and shame. Yet, in our guilt, we sense our fragility, the limits of what we can endure. At that point we may well go silent. Our soul turns deaf and dumb. Speech ceases. No longer can words express our remorse and self-condemnation. We cannot even describe our wounds.

In the very worst moments, life itself seems to leave and the soul seems to go dead, like an empty tomb. The light goes out of our eyes. The inner energy that once signaled hope and a belief in ourselves fades, yielding to the infinite, empty grayness around us.

But when we have gone numb, when we have confronted the worst within us with honesty, when we have been bared to the soul, then the return can begin. Yes, we are ready to collapse altogether. But at that moment, another possibility arises.

Into the grayness grace can come. The light that has gone out can be rekindled by a light from outside, a piercing brightness that can burn away all the shadows and dross of our corrupted reality. In the crucible of confession, hope can be forged once more.

> Lord, all my longing is known to thee,
>   my sighing is not hidden from thee. . . .
> I confess my iniquity,
>   I am sorry for my sin. . . .
> Do not forsake me, O LORD!
>   O my God, be not far from me!
> Make haste to help me,
>   O Lord, my salvation!
>
> Psalm 38:9, 18, 21-22

5

Chastened

Remove thy stroke from me;
 I am spent by the blows of thy hand.
When thou dost chasten [us]
 with rebukes for sin,
thou dost consume like a moth what is dear to [us];
 surely every [one of us] is a mere breath!

Psalm 39:10-11

"Chastened" is an old-fashioned word. But in times of defeat it can take on fresh meaning. To be chastened is to feel the sting of rebuke or discipline and to know quite well why it is given. To a degree, it is cleansing. By accepting chastening we balance the scales as we begin to atone for our guilt, to pay the price of our wrongdoing.

Often it seems harsh—there is a limit to what we feel we can endure. We reach the point where we are spent by the blows of the chastener. Usually that is well beyond where we ourselves would have declared the blows sufficient, based on our own scales of justice.

Normally we would prefer that the discipline stop short of actually hurting us. We would rather that it not penetrate our protective walls, that it not touch us where we are most vulnerable, where we might have to experience the same kind of pain that we have caused others.

We are afraid of pain because we have known its effect. We don't doubt that others have known it too. We may even acknowledge that their pain is partly our fault. But do we have to experience it too? Is the causing of equal pain in return the only way to offset the injuries sustained? Unfortunately, most people think so; yet sometimes the pain we experience goes beyond chastening, beyond discipline, beyond balancing the scales, beyond even revenge. Sometimes we feel consumed: "Thou dost consume like a moth what is dear to [us]" (Ps 39:11b).

To be so consumed is to come to the edge of annihilation. It is to lose not only what is dear—job, home, marriage, reputation—but in the process to come close to losing our reason for existence as well. When we are rebuked and consumed by the forces around us, when we lose those relationships and structures that have been the basic motivations for our life, then we feel what it is to be a "mere breath" on this planet. Existence itself comes into question, and we struggle with whether we should continue to live at all.

Where are we left when we come to such a point? What motive remains for pressing on? The psalmist appealed to God:

> "Look away from me, that I may know gladness,
> before I depart and be no more!"
>
> Psalm 39:13

The author just wanted to be left alone for a while to glean whatever fragments of happiness might be salvaged. We understand that feeling, that desire for relief and a space in which to lick our wounds. But the psalmist raises another question.

Causes

No matter how our trial begins—whether we are discovered in wrongdoing, caught in a web of our own making, or even falsely accused—is it all simply a product of our own fallibility and that of others? Or does it have a wider dimension? Could our rebuke be an act of God?

To one who is a believer, the question of God's involvement is profoundly important. For if God has a hand in the personal undoing and chastening of one's existence, there must be a meaning at stake that urgently needs to be considered.

But there is another possibility. There is the possibility of the dark side, of powers and principalities, of hostile forces that seek to undo and destroy us. Some people would call it "Satan." Others see it as a manifestation of unresolved conflicts deep within the human subconscious. However it is understood, the possibility is real that the tragedies of our lives may not be simply a matter of personal failure but of larger forces at work.

That is both a scary and a comforting thought. We are and should be afraid of forces greater than ourselves, whether those forces are demonic, divine, psychological, or social. For to be blind toward such possibilities, to assume that all aspects of our lives are subject to our own control, is an almost certain step toward disaster. No matter how self-confident we may be, no matter how insulated by wealth or power, we need to retain a healthy sense of that which is beyond us. Life is always greater than we are.

To acknowledge external forces has a comforting side. It gives us something to blame. That can be bad if it is a way of avoiding responsibility for our own failures.

But it can also bring relief. By recognizing the external forces in our fall, we can recover the control necessary for forging ahead. We then become able to distinguish between what is unhealthy and what is upbuilding. We may also find common ground on which to stand with others. We may find company to help in redressing our woes, rebuilding our lives, and resisting further onslaughts of whatever would destroy us.

God, Satan, or simply the natural consequences of our choices—these are all places to look in coming to understand how we got where we are. It can be difficult to discern which of these forces are at play. Our fall may come from a combination of all three.

Only God, however, carries the promise of a future redeemed. For when God is experienced as a participant in the chastening, there is also the vision of One who is powerful and loving enough to turn the chastening into something good and to move us beyond it to something new.

> And now, Lord, for what do I wait?
> My hope is in thee.
> Deliver me from all my transgressions.
>
> Psalm 39:7-8

6

Abandoned

O LORD, my God, I call for help by day;
  I cry out in the night before thee. . . .
For my soul is full of troubles,. . .
  I am a man who has no strength,
like one forsaken among the dead,
  like the slain that lie in the grave. . . .
Thou hast put me in the depths of the Pit,
  in the regions dark and deep. . . .
I am shut in so that I cannot escape;
  my eye grows dim through sorrow. . . .
O LORD, why dost thou cast me off?
  Why dost thou hide thy face from me?
Afflicted and close to death from my youth up,
  I suffer thy terrors; I am helpless.
Thy wrath has swept over me;
  thy dread assaults destroy me. . . .
Thou hast caused lover and friend to shun me.

Psalm 88:1, 3, 4b, 5a, 6, 8b, 9a, 14-16, 18

Among all the cries of the psalmist this is the most desolate. This cry remains unanswered. There is no happy ending here—not even the promise of one.

There are other psalms of abandonment in Scripture. Psalm 22, for example, begins with the well-known words that Jesus spoke from the cross, "My God, my God, why hast thou forsaken me?" and continues with a heartbreaking picture of what it feels like to be abandoned. But then the psalm turns around, finishing on a note of triumph and confidence in God's power to deliver.

Psalm 88 does not turn around. In this most desolate psalm of all, there is no deliverance. There is only the cry, the despair, and the darkness. When our cries go unanswered, are we not devastated? There is such emptiness in not being heard. It means that we are alone, stuck in our terrible isolation. How can there be meaning when our suffering goes unrecognized and our existence goes unnoticed?

Suffering, to have meaning, needs a context. It requires that we be connected to others who value our existence and what we experience. One of the common marks of desolation, in this psalm as well as others, is being cut off from companionship, losing connection with peers, family, community. To not be in relationship is to approach extinction.

In this psalm even the relationship with God is called into question. The psalmist cries to God repeatedly, but there is no answer. Instead there is the endless pain. "Afflicted and close to death from youth up," the psalmist knew the weight of long-term suffering.

We can identify with such a cry. Whether plagued by long-term disease or crippled by patterns learned as children of dysfunctional families, we understand the power of the past. We know how inner afflictions can stay with us for years, sometimes hidden, able to suddenly rear their horned heads and gore our lives to shreds.

These unresolved demons of the past do not lose their power. They may even become stronger as time passes. Until they are exorcised, we, like the psalmist, feel trapped, shut in, unable to escape.

We learn the meaning of the Pit, where one is neither dead nor alive. There we are cut off, surrounded by a gloom that no light can penetrate. There is nothing for which to be thankful.

When we come to the Pit, hurling our cries into the void, we meet life's deepest mystery. We discover places in the soul where no peace can be found, where life remains cloaked with darkness.

Standing at the edge of this abyss, the psalmist appealed finally to God's self-interest:

Do the shades rise up to praise thee?
　Is thy steadfast love declared in the grave . . . ?
Are thy wonders known in the darkness,
　or thy saving help in the land of forgetfulness?

Psalm 88:10b, 11a, 12

Still there was silence. The psalm ends unresolved, as do many pieces of our lives.

How, then, do we find comfort in these words? Do they not leave us even more disturbed?

Perhaps there is comfort in having the psalm the way it is. The cry is left hanging, unresolved. For us, the grace is in the fact that this unanswered cry exists, in all its naked despair. God, who has given us these words, allows us the authenticity of our own desolation.

There are certainly times when the pain needs to stand as it is. To disguise it would be treason against the soul. Always there are those who would bandage our wounds and cover them over with saccharine cliches. But these people hide only their own insecurities. To stand naked in our deepest agony is to discover a necessary part of ourselves, perhaps of the universe.

In the end, the terrible end, we may come only to silence. We, too, are left unresolved. It seems beyond human capability to remain indefinitely in this limbo, but for a while, we must touch the impenetrable silence.

Is it a holy silence? Does the silence create a sacred space? a space for survival? a necessary space—one of those crucibles of the soul in which we are melted down for remolding? Or is it an unholy, frightening space?

O LORD, why dost thou cast me off?

Psalm 88:14

7

Silence

For my days pass away like smoke,
* and my bones burn like a furnace.*
My heart is smitten like grass, and withered;
* I forget to eat my bread.*
Because of my loud groaning
* my bones cleave to my flesh. . . .*
I lie awake,
* I am like a lonely bird on the housetop. . . .*
For I eat ashes like bread,
* and mingle tears with my drink,*
because of thy indignation and anger;
* for thou hast taken me up and thrown me away.*
My days are like an evening shadow;
* I wither away like grass.*

Hear my prayer, O LORD;
* let my cry come to thee!*
Do not hide thy face from me
* in the day of my distress!*

Psalm 102:3-5, 7, 9-11, 1-2a

What sorrowful words! What lonely words! Such pathos is gathered in these achings of the heart! In them is captured the emptiness and inner weariness that affliction brings.

The image in the opening words of this passage reminds us of another human experience—the destroying furnaces of the concentration camps of World War II where human beings were literally, obscenely consumed by flames of fanaticism. We must be careful how we use such imagery out of respect for those who understand it so much more profoundly and tragically than we do. But we may each come, in our own life, to personal holocausts. These will hardly be as extreme, as undeserved, or as shockingly incomprehensible as that historical reality. But the chaos and destruction that results can be personally devastating. They can torment and consume us, evoking our deepest anguish and most powerful emotions. They can bring loss and change that may last a lifetime.

In this image of days passing like smoke, of burning bones and a withered heart, we sense the bottomless sorrow of which the human soul is capable, so all-embracing that it can even take physical form. When the appetite for life disintegrates, so does the appetite for the very food that sustains us. Why bother to preserve the body when the soul has collapsed? So, too, sleep evades us. We lie awake in restless turmoil wishing for the escape that unconsciousness will bring. Physically and figuratively, those things that once gave us nourishment and pleasure become ashes in the mouth, bitter and worthless.

Life loses its flavor. Motivation disappears. There is an emptiness of the soul that immobilizes us and reduces all of life to dismal dreariness.

In these days that seem like deep twilight there is an unending gloom. Even the brightest moments have shadows. In the background an ominous, darkening cloud waits, ready to blot out whatever relief or joy we might find. As grass withers, so too does our spirit fade. Life drains away, leaving us brittle and brown. We become like a creature perched high on a rooftop, looking down on the unfolding tragedy yet feeling distant, disconnected, detached. Life goes on around us but not in us.

It is a very lonely feeling. To be cut off from those closest to us is bad enough. To be cut off even from ourselves is worse still. Eventually we may come to feel, as the psalmist did, like worthless garbage, discarded and forgotten. There is no self-esteem left.

Consolation

Perhaps the consolation in these words is that they are spoken at all. That enough breath remains in the soul to give voice to these dispirited sighs is itself a glimmer of promise. Despite the emptiness and anguish the psalmist feels, there is enough of a sense of loss to deliberately record the bitter experience. By etching this sorrow in the cold walls of eternity, the psalm writer declares a belief in the value of being itself, as well as a belief in better possibilities.

Of course, these are the words of a believer, one who hopes in a God who can save. As the psalm begins, the writer appeals to a God who seems hidden: "Do not hide thy face from me" (Ps 102:2a). These are critical words. For if God withdraws, if God abandons us, then few possibilities for salvation remain. "O my God, be not far from me" (Ps 38:21b) is a common psalm cry. For a God far away, removed, is a God who will neither hear us nor respond. Our hope, in the psalmist's view, is that God will be near, will be Immanuel, God-with-us.

These images of God "far" versus God "near," of God hidden versus God present, are profoundly important. Many believers have experienced "the dark night of the soul," those periods when God seems hidden or gone altogether. One of the most grueling tests of the human spirit is to enter into such a time and to emerge with faith intact.

It is precisely at that point that many people determine faith to be a delusion. If God does not answer—so goes the reasoning—then God must not be. Or if God is and chooses not to respond, then such a God does not deserve loyalty and respect. Held to human standards, God comes up short.

Yet there are other standards, other views and experiences, that can lead people to cry to God even against God's silence. They hold God accountable, but to God's own standards of mercy, faithfulness, and justice as experienced in history. There is no judgment made of God—God is still viewed as the truth beyond understanding.

> I kept my faith, even when I said,
> "I am greatly afflicted."
>
> Psalm 116:10

Submission and Self-Affirmation

Such a believer was the psalmist. After this litany of sorrow and abandonment, after recounting this profound experience of desolation and grief, the psalmist turns a hundred and eighty degrees with four words: "But, thou, O Lord . . . " (Ps 102:12a).

Yes, the psalmist's life is forfeit. His world has collapsed, and there is nothing left to turn it around. Moreover, that does not matter much anymore. But then, the psalmist bows like Job to the sheer sovereignty of God, letting go of personal reality and focusing on a greater reality.

As the rest of the psalm unfolds, the psalmist becomes absorbed in an ever-wider story, one that takes into account the sufferings and joys of many other people and acknowledges that life, indeed, the universe itself, is ultimately temporary. Whatever is reality as we know it will pass. Nothing endures forever, save God.

Yet there is a glimmer of self-affirmation, a charming appeal to the value of even one life in the midst of this cosmic drama:

> "O my God," I say, "take me not hence
> in the midst of my days,
> thou whose years endure
> throughout all generations!"
>
> Psalm 102:24

There is a selfish but distinctly human logic in this plea: "What difference does it make to you, O God, if I get a few more years of life—you who have an unlimited supply?"

But there is also inspiration for us and hope in this appeal to the Creator to validate one broken, human life for just a little longer, out of sheer grace. Even a miserable life has hope for healing and is to be preferred to obliteration. That will come soon enough in any case.

In these ways hope remains. There is redemption in that this desolate cry may be spoken at all. Our own experiences of sorrow and emptiness are validated by the existence of words like these.

There is hope, too, in the larger context, for we belong to a whole community of people who know what it is to suffer. In the still-unfolding cosmic drama the full meaning of our lives and of suffering itself will become clear as we are absorbed into a greater destiny than we can now comprehend.

But for now, we may rightfully plead our cause and make our hurts known. In fact, we must, because not to do so is to risk diminishing ourselves altogether. Our hearts need to speak in times of sorrow as well as joy, and when they do, we ourselves need to listen.

8

Time

How long, O LORD? Wilt thou forget me forever?
  How long wilt thou hide thy face from me?
How long must I bear pain in my soul,
  and have sorrow in my heart all the day?
How long shall my enemy be exalted over me?

Psalm 13:1–2

Times of affliction can seem interminable. There is an endless, all-consuming quality to them. Sometimes it feels as if the rest of one's life will be spent under the curse of failure and tragedy. The thought of a future unrelieved by forgiveness or change weighs with terminal heaviness upon the soul.

We are creatures born for freedom. Having grown up in a culture that saturates us with images of change and self-determination, we are not easily reconciled to long periods of imprisonment, even when deserved. By nature we are inclined to believe in alternatives; we fight fatalism and are constantly envisioning a future.

It is this sense of a future that gives us incentive for the present. Hope itself is premised on the assumption of alternative possibilities. Whether one is Christian or not, the story of Jesus' resurrection captivates us because it images for us one of our most treasured dreams—liberation from the tombs of our lives both in the present and in the future.

Affliction is a form of tomb existence. And we long for release because there lives in our soul a yearning for resurrection from the failures and flaws that enshroud our lives. Indeed, it is a profound comment on the nature of our humanity that we have this capacity called hope in the first place, that we dare to dream beyond our own imperfections. Yet even as we long for new possibilities, we are restrained by the grave clothes of our failure.

We need it to end. We need to come to a moment when we are freed from the past, when we can lay down the loads we carry and walk away, leaving them behind.

For some people that comes easily. They learn to do it naturally or with the help of others. Some do it through prayer. Others are never in a position to let go completely and walk away but may at least come to a point where their minds are free and their consciences relieved.

Endings are both necessary and helpful. They represent a process of death and resurrection. They enable new beginnings. One of the sweetest experiences of life is to be relieved of a burden and to receive a completely fresh opportunity to live out the hopes within us. Through such experiences we learn the meaning of grace.

All this does not ignore the fact that sometimes we deserve our afflictions, that we have violated those norms of conduct designed to protect ourselves and others in the human community. Our afflictions may well reflect accountability for personal misdeeds.

But without limits, afflictions lose their value. Interminable affliction is an affront to human dignity, and with no possibility for resolution, life and human community as a whole are reduced in quality and purpose.

In the end, afflictions are best understood as comments about the past or a past that is about to be. Allen Wheelis, in Chapter 1 of *How People Change,* uses the image of a thief to describe the distinction between past failures and future possibilities. For one to be called a thief may be a statement of fact, but it is not a statement about one's destiny. A thief may be what one was, but the future is open to alternative possibilities.*

We need to learn better how to separate the person from the act when it comes to both bad and good deeds. Obviously, being and behavior are integrally related. But that does not mean they

*Allen Wheelis, *How People Change,* (New York: Harper & Row, 1973).

are identical. There is in each of us room for alteration of the relationship between being and behavior. Bad fruit will certainly come from a bad tree and good fruit from a good tree. But even trees can be pruned and nurtured so as to correct and improve their harvest.

Yet people are not trees! Each of us is an intricate set of interacting factors. And within each person lie possibilities for different futures eventually compelling us to cry, "How long, O Lord?"

It is the spirit of resurrection within us that gives birth to those words. We are imbued with a sense of purpose and value, and we are set in a context where those qualities and the questions they produce are meaningful. That sense of purpose, that spirit that cries "How long?" is part of the matrix of life. That we even care "how long" is a confirmation of our worth.

9

Salvation

Save me, O God!

Psalm 69:1a

Turn, O LORD, save my life.

Psalm 6:4a

Redeem Israel, O God,
 out of all [trouble].

Psalm 25:22

Some of our cries—perhaps all of them—are for salvation. Why? What do we mean by salvation? Why does this desire arise within us in the first place?

In the biblical context salvation is associated with God—it is one of the things God does. In that respect, the biblical God is hardly unique. All religions speak of some kind of salvation, of deliverance from burdens, conflicts, even from life itself.

But what is it to be saved? What do we desire when we seek this thing called salvation? What does our need tell us about who we are and how we see life?

First of all, of course, salvation means a change from our immediate circumstances. We want to get out of whatever trouble we are in. When we are faced with the consequences of our wrongdoing, to be saved means simply to escape, even from just penalties, or to get off with a lesser penalty than we deserve.

It may even mean total absolution, being set free from the consequences of our actions by someone who trusts us not to repeat them, as we may have learned as children. As adults, we are supposed to have learned accountability. Yet, when crises arrive, the child within us longs for release. Unfortunately, we will seldom find such release in the grown-up world for there we have become too hardened.

Sometimes being saved means being delivered from the consequences of our wrongdoing through a process of self-examination, therapy, external accountability, support systems, or whatever else is required to help us overcome self-destructive or socially destructive patterns. Salvation in that perspective may continue to unfold over a long period of time.

Most often, however, we picture salvation as something immediate—as relief from current struggles or pain. If we are honest with ourselves, we know that what we often desire is for life to be restored to the way it was before the trouble began. We want to go back to comfortable patterns.

In this respect, our desire for salvation reflects a fundamental selfishness. We all want the world to continue revolving around the patterns and choices we have selected for ordering our lives, for protecting ourselves, and for giving us what we think will bring satisfaction.

But on a deeper level, the desire for salvation is an affirmation of life and of ourselves. It says that we value both. One of our deepest and most profound capabilities is this capacity to affirm and value ourselves, each other, our experiences together, and life itself. Therefore it is only natural that when our lives and relationships are marred or destroyed—for whatever reason—we feel hurt. In itself, that is a positive sign of our inner quality and potential. But only rarely do we see salvation as a movement toward changed attitudes, changed actions, changed choices. We are usually afraid of change and of exposing ourselves to the risks that change entails, especially when self-esteem is already low or hard won.

But salvation eventually does involve us in change by causing us to face our vulnerabilities. That is what crises are all about. They bring us to our breaking points. They expose our finitude. In that process they show us new meanings of salvation.

When the heaviest, most profound crises arrive in our lives, they push us beyond the more primitive images of salvation. Truly severe crises have a way of stripping us to the bone psychologically, spiritually, even physically. At that point we may come to realize that salvation is something that must finally come from outside. For ultimately, salvation involves us in an experience beyond what we have known so far, a reality greater than ourselves.

Whether we find that reality to be God, as the psalmists did, or a deeper kind of self-discovery or something different still, salvation will turn out to be much more than mere escape. At its fullest, salvation enlarges us and opens the door to altogether new possibilities.

Justice Expected

Along the way, salvation tells us something about our being. As our troubles unfold and our cries for salvation surface, we reconnect with an aspect of ourselves that ordinarily goes unnoticed: Deep within us we have a sense that life should be otherwise than troubled, destroyed, or filled with conflict. When our world comes crashing down, when we see suffering around us or feel bruises within, an inner voice speaks to us saying that life was not meant to be this way. Where does that inborn consciousness come from?

What we feel when we are injured is more than animal pain. As humans we have a sense of justice violated that disturbs us, both when our own lives are injured and, if we are healthy, when we see injuries to others. Programmed deep within our minds and souls is a curious awareness of what should or should not be. When something is wrong we know it. Guilt, conscience, convictions about fairness—these are all outgrowths of that inborn consciousness. Whether it comes from God or is a supreme manifestation of millennia of human social development, it exists.

So strong is this sense of good and bad, right and wrong, harmony and disharmony, that for most of us, it drives us to protest unsatisfactory situations and to seek remedies. Implicitly, we believe in alternatives. Deeper than our ability to screw up is our desire not to, or at least to live a life not tortured by our own fallibility.

Call it the Genesis Syndrome—that description of human origins and failure given in the opening chapters of Scripture. Already in this early account of human existence that seeks to describe our very beginnings—already there do we discern the vision of life as it should be and of life in its brokenness.

The order is important. In the Genesis account the ideal comes first. Corruption follows. What that means is that behind our experiences of disaster is already a dream of life unbroken, perfect, without failure.

But we are out of the garden now and still eating the forbidden fruit. Our endless striving to be as gods continues to warp and unbalance our lives, returning us again and again to shame, to knowing our own nakedness. We come back to the cry, the cry for salvation, the call to someone or something outside that can give us deliverance. We still cover ourselves with assorted fig leaves, afraid of being discovered yet longing for reconciliation, healing, and hope.

In the Garden story of Genesis, there was a judgment and discipline following the Fall. But even before discipline there was an image of salvation. There was the coming of the Creator, walking calmly into the now-broken world. The Almighty One came not in fury and condemnation but speaking words of connection and concern: "Where are you?"

God could have exercised the powers of all-knowing and blasted the fallen couple with a radar-like strike. Instead, Scripture presents a God who chooses to come into the brokenness gently, in person, with respect for those whom God has made, despite their failure. Though God is personally wounded by this sorry breach of trust, God does not break the relationship that has begun. God judges, but God does not abandon. Instead God provides protection and, later, a promise—a promise of salvation.

It is to this kind of God that the psalmists continually appeal. In their brokenness they cry—not on the basis of their own deserving but on the basis of this external possibility of salvation. The grounds for their appeal is not in themselves but in a greater reality.

> Answer me, O LORD, for thy steadfast love is good;
> according to thy abundant mercy, turn to me. . . .
> Turn, O LORD, save my life;
> deliver me for the sake of thy steadfast love.
>
> Psalm 6:4

10

Prayer

I cry aloud to God,
  aloud to God, that [God] may hear me.
In the day of my trouble I seek the Lord;
  in the night my hand is stretched out without wearying;
  my soul refuses to be comforted. . . .
I think of God, and I moan;
  I meditate, and my spirit faints. . . .
I am so troubled that I cannot speak.
Will the Lord spurn for ever . . . ?
Has [God's] steadfast love for ever ceased?
  Are [God's] promises at an end for all time?
Has God forgotten to be gracious?
  Has [God] in anger shut up [all] compassion? . . .

  Psalm 77:1-3, 4b, 7a, 8-9

Be not silent, O God of my praise!

  Psalm 109:1

The lifeline of hope is communication. To be out of touch, cut off, isolated, disconnected from the sources of our survival, is a most perilous state. As the awareness grows within us of the threat to our being, we engage whatever resources we can just to hang on.

One stage of survival is prayer—passionate, persistent, even angry prayer. Prayer focuses the cry within—the cry that arises when the mind is about to burst from the pressures building up around and inside us. Prayer translates the agonies of the heart into a manageable form, into a deliberate if sometimes desperate plea for an explanation, for some response to the turmoil in which we find ourselves. We want to understand what is happening to us and to vent our frustration over it.

As the psalmist puts it, our soul refuses to be comforted. We insist that God respond, that someone, at least, recognize the churning emotions within us. We need to vent.

At the same time our prayers can feel blocked. The anger that wells up within can obstruct the very pain we need to express. Shock, fear, and self-condemnation can render our prayer ineffective and leave us feeling still trapped in the maelstrom.

We feel so unworthy. How dare we implore God to listen or to help? Our heart pleads for understanding and compassion, yet we are so confused that we hardly know what to plead or whether we are justified in making any plea at all. The surrounding realities overwhelm the senses and distort the ability to think clearly. What is truth? What is real? Truth and reality seem to shift with each passing day. A cold, sickly hopelessness invades the spirit.

Still and more than ever we cry. At those points of the most anguish, confusion, and uncertainty, at the very edge of the threatening abyss, our soul sends forth its relentless prayer.

But in return comes the silence—that wrenching, oppressive, bitter quiet where we had expected and even demanded to hear the voice of God. A God who is so unresponsive is such a disturbing God. This silence leaves us cold, puzzled, still stuck in our hurt and wondering why we even bothered to believe or to pray. If doubt does not overtake us, anger may. Why does God not respond? How can God offer such promises of comfort and love, yet remain silent in the face of our suffering? Our diatribes may finally yield to patience and to the rationalization or belief that God will act in due time. But in the meantime, a bitter taste and a heaviness of heart remain.

At least these psalm words tell us that we are not the first to raise our sighs before a silent God. We are not the first to be frustrated when no response is forthcoming. And we are clearly not alone in feeling angry over our plight, even if that plight is of our own making.

Nor are we the only ones who have moaned in the very depths of our being over shattered dreams, broken relationships, and the disappointment of crying out to the One we trusted to help us, only to receive an inadequate reply. We are in the great, sad company of those who have felt alone in the darkness—abandoned, dissatisfied, and troubled by the silence. Perhaps knowing that can bring at least temporary relief.

11

Remembrance

Will the Lord spurn forever,
and never again be favorable?

Psalm 77:7

There are days when no hope remains, when no redemption is in sight. "Spurn" becomes no longer only a word but a tangible state, a living reality that diminishes our existence. The thought of never being restored, of life never returning to normal, is one of the most dismal prospects we can face. It saps the soul's instinct for life itself.

But we are human beings; we must live with promise. Something about the human spirit requires that we believe in alternative possibilities. Without hope, we dry up into shadows of what we were meant to be, pale silhouettes of the possibilities within us.

The psalmist found relief and recovered hope in two key ways. First, the psalmist appealed to God's own identity, to what it means to be God. Then, the psalmist turned to memory.

God

Has God forgotten to be gracious?
Had [God] in anger shut up [all] compassion?

Psalm 77:9

According to Scripture, it is God's nature to be gracious and show compassion. But how does the psalmist, a mere mortal, dare

49

to challenge God? Is it not impertinent to call God to such account? to even hint that the Almighty could fail to exercise this fundamental dimension of God's being?

Even though the psalmist suggests that God's anger at human failure justifies the withdrawal of God's compassion, the indictment remains. Perhaps, too, the psalmist is voicing how it feels to stand before the darkness with no promise of a light ahead.

For a believer in the God of Scripture, to be fully faithful means to bow before the sovereignty of the Almighty, to accept even the silence of God. It is also to recognize that nothing is more horrible than the utter desolation of being cut off forever from the possibility of grace, forgiveness, and renewal.

Memory

Standing before this void, the psalmist had but one recourse— to claim the memories that can renew a sense of hope: "I will call to mind the deeds of the LORD" (Ps 77:11).

When we come to the bleakness, when our cries fall into the void and no voice echoes our longing, where is there left for us to go?

Memories are one of our best resources. A retreat into the mind is one place to flee for refuge and healing, at least for a time. For no matter how destructive the forces outside may become, there are spheres inside that endure and provide strength. Through memory we can touch what is reliable and concrete. When we are surrounded by the uncertain, memory can be a comforting realm of the known.

Yet even there we must be on guard. For it is also true that the most insidious attacks are those against the mind itself. There are people whose betrayals and changes of heart lead them to attempt to rewrite the past, to revise it into a version that better suits their own agendas. Such attacks undermine our ability to trust ourselves as well as others. But in our memories, we can find the necessary facts and reference points to establish stability, at least for surviving the current crisis.

Of course, from time to time we need to reexamine the past, to sift through it in new ways for new insights. Sometimes we will see old experiences differently. But we must also cling to the certainties we find there because, for better or worse, they are who we are, or, at least, who we were at given points in our lives.

Remembering past affirmations can encourage us in the present. Recalling those people and events that have defined us usually renews our sense of identity and inspires us to hang on, as they did, in times of crisis. Such memories remind us that we are part of a much greater reality. Finally, such memories teach us about ourselves, clarifying those persistent qualities within us—both good and bad—that can aid our survival and recovery.

There is strength in memory. And if remembering brings a renewed sense of constancy in our lives, a sense of progress and of grace in our past, then there is great encouragement for surviving the crisis of the present with a solid hope for the future.

> I will call to mind the deeds of the LORD;
> yea, I will remember thy wonders of old.
>
> Psalm 77:11

Part II
Words of Adversity

Introduction: Enemy Times

O LORD, how many are my foes!
Many are rising against me.

Psalm 3:1

Deliver me from my enemies, O my God,
protect me from those who rise up against me.

Psalm 59:1

It is one of the tragedies of human conflict that people become enemies. "Enemy" is a strong term. But it vividly describes the extent of hostility that can arise when we become alienated from one another.

Enemies exist. They may be only vague projections we attach to those who are different from us—racially, politically, religiously, and so on. Or they may be flesh-and-blood individuals who mean to do us harm. Either way, they evoke strong emotions, affecting our lives in significant ways.

We may be more comfortable with abstract, distant enemies than with close-up ones. So ominous do we find the very word "enemy" that we may prefer to use it only vaguely. To apply it to persons with whom we experience conflict can bring more tension into the relationship. For enemy implies the impossibility of reconciliation. An enemy is one from whom we must be permanently polarized. Enemies are to be avoided or destroyed lest they bring destruction to us.

Clearly, "enemy" is a potent term and one to be used carefully. But it is also a dynamic term. Used cautiously, it might free us to name what wounds us and to vent the wrath that lives with such strong power inside us. Used wisely, the word "enemy" might even open doors for reconciliation.

In the psalms there are nearly fifty references to personal enemies. The psalmists were not afraid to use this concept to describe their experiences. Of course, those were different days. The psalm writers lived in an age when enemies often came literally bearing arms with an intent to punish and destroy. The inner description had an outer reality.

Yet it is clear that there is also a very different kind of enemy situation in the psalms. Sometimes one's enemies are friends or peers. The psalms show us the very real and tragic consequences that follow when relationships break down and people who once were partners turn against each other.

We have experienced that kind of sad and painful development ourselves often enough to relate to the psalmist's story. Perhaps we would rather describe those who somehow stand over against us as adversaries rather than as full-fledged enemies. Yet "enemy" language is presented for us throughout the psalms. By employing this term, by facing it squarely and seeing how it functioned for the psalm writers, we might find helpful guidance for ourselves.

It would be a sad consequence if our understanding of the term "enemy" caused us to divide the people we know into enemies and friends. That would be a misappropriation of the term and would bring us harm instead of benefit. But there may be ways in which the term "enemy" can clarify our experiences, crystallize our emotions, and help us to vent and examine the feelings that arise in times of adversity. With that awareness of its limited usefulness, we can pursue the value in thinking in "enemy" terms.

12

Contention

Contend, O LORD, with those who contend against me;
  fight against those who fight against me! . . .
Draw the spear and javelin
  against my pursuers!
Say to my soul,
  "I am your deliverance!"
Let them be put to shame and dishonor
  who seek after my life! . . .
Let their way be dark and slippery. . . .
For without cause they hid their net for me.

Psalm 35:1, 3, 4a, 6a, 7a

Malicious witnesses rise up;
  they ask me of things that I know not.
They requite me evil for good;
  my soul is forlorn. . . .
But at my stumbling they gathered in glee.

Psalm 35:11, 12, 15a

Vindicate me, O LORD, my God,
  according to thy righteousness. . . .
Let those who desire my vindication
  shout for joy and be glad,
  and say evermore,
"Great is the LORD,
  who delights in the welfare of [God's] servant!"

Then my tongue shall tell of thy righteousness
and of thy praise all the day long.

Psalm 35:24a, 27, 28

These are fighting words. They are words of passion that portray a highly charged situation. In these words we find four basic reactions to conflict: (1) typical conflict mentality, (2) intense anger at one's accusers, (3) mournful indication of the inner dimensions and effects of conflict, and (4) appeal for vindication and relief.

Fighting

On the surface, the appeal to God in the beginning of this passage might seem to be no more than that. But it reveals those deeper emotions that the conflict has already produced. For the writer of this psalm doesn't just ask for help. The psalmist asks for spears and shields—weapons and an attack. This writer is already deeply engaged in an emotionally charged conflict. The first thought here is not to retreat or negotiate. It is to fight.

Such a battle mentality is instinctive when we enter into conflict situations. One of our first reactions is to want to strike back. Even when we are attacked for good reason, we resist and move toward counterattack.

Why is that? Where did we get that tendency? Is it the self-preservation instinct, left over from primitive days when resistance was required for survival? Or does it reflect the darker side within us, that Cain-and-Abel mentality that breeds conflict out of jealousies and a destructive kind of competitiveness?

Whom are we fighting when we engage in personal battles? Is it always an unjustified accuser or someone who has wronged us? Or are we directing at others some of the inner hostility we feel over our own failures and fears? Does our dread of vulnerability and powerlessness cause us to direct our frustrations outward in an attempt to find release for the struggles of our own soul? Do we hope to cover over apparent inner conflicts by finding some surrogate to do battle with? The dynamics of conflict are more complex than we realize.

In choosing to fight, one of the first things we look for is help. We rush to rally our resources for defending ourselves and for pressing the attack.

> Take hold of shield and buckler,
>   and rise for my help!
>
> Psalm 35:2

So cries the psalmist. In this image God is made out to be a kind of cosmic gladiator who will physically enter the battle to protect and fight for the one accused. While the image is a captivating one, reminiscent of a John Wayne movie where the hero comes rushing to the rescue, it also reflects a deeper truth. The basic reality is, we do not want to fight alone. Both the possibility of losing and the prospect of fighting alone are depressing. We feel much braver when someone fights at our side.

On so many occasions in life what we need is an advocate. To go through trials without any voice to speak on our behalf is one of life's most miserable experiences. So basic is this need that we recognize it as a legal right in our judicial system. Yet there are times and places in our lives where no advocate appears—or none is allowed. Our fundamental need for that companion voice goes unfulfilled. We are left unprotected, untempered, alone. At such a time, we discover how bleak life can be.

In turning to God, the psalmist seeks an advocate. There is even an appeal to God's underdog instinct:

> All my bones shall say,
>   "O LORD, who is like thee,
> thou who deliverest the weak
>   from [those] who [are] too strong for [them],
> the weak and needy from [those] who [despoil them]?"
>
> Psalm 35:10

The psalmist seeks assurance that there is some hope of prevailing in this conflict. A hint of the inner anxiety that gnaws away at even the most confident soul comes through in the psalmist's appeal.

> Say to my soul,
> "I am your deliverance!"
>
> Psalm 35:3b

We want reassurance in the midst of conflict. We want to know that we will prevail or at least survive. We reach out wherever we can for help, especially for those resources that have helped us in the past.

It is good that we have this survival instinct in times of conflict and that it pushes us to reach out for connections with people and resources beyond ourselves. Even when our cause is not just, through reaching out we can receive strength for surviving long enough to perceive and acknowledge our errors. At best, the connections we make lead us beyond conflict to better times and relationships ahead.

Anger

> Let their way be dark and slippery,
> with the angel of the LORD, pursuing them! . . .
> Let ruin come upon them unawares!
> And let the net which they hid ensnare them;
> let them fall therein to ruin!
>
> Psalm 35:6, 8

Anger is a major dimension of conflict. Often it rises to the fore more swiftly and remains the most visibly dominant of all our reactions. Even when justified, personal attacks have a way of stirring up within us powerful, often vitriolic responses.

One way we focus anger is in curses, visions of our adversaries encountering mishap or suffering similar to ours—preferably, worse. Unquestionably, there is a dark side to such longings. They reveal the nastier side of our soul; they reflect just how distorted and vindictive our perspective can become.

Such imaginings also serve other functions that may not be all bad. For one thing, they bring our feelings to the surface and help us to vent our anger. Anger denied can explode in worse ways than in curses: When we try to repress or control such intense feelings, they inevitably pop out in some other, perhaps more destructive, manner.

There is, of course, a certain danger in our evil wishes toward our adversaries. At worst, we might actualize the fantasy and translate ill wishes into ill actions.

At best, however, fantasizing—even fantasizing harm—is preferable to the actual commission of it. By pronouncing such anathemas we get in touch with the intensity of our emotions. At the same time we create a release valve for much of the negative energy within us. It may not be one of our most edifying coping mechanisms, but it is one of the most common and practicable ones. One day we may learn to respond with grace and forgiveness when attacked or accused. Until then, we have anger. If we use it carefully, it will consume neither us nor others.

Accusation

> Malicious witnesses rise up;
>> they ask me of things that I know not. . . .
> For without cause they hid their net for me;
>> without cause they dug a pit for my life. . . .
> They requite me evil for good;
>> my soul is forlorn. . . .
> But at my stumbling they gathered in glee.
>> Psalm 35:11, 7, 12, 15a

Beneath the anger there is often deep hurt. When one is falsely accused, the personal wounds are particularly painful. There is injury to one's pride as one's integrity is called into question. There is also the frustration of not understanding why others would undertake such attacks or level such charges. What has gone wrong? Why are they doing this? What has changed?

The pain is compounded by the humiliation and implied guilt that accusations bring. For accusations are never neutral pronouncements. They have a life of their own. Once launched, they fly toward the target and explode around it in ways that set off waves of innuendo, suspicion, and embarrassment.

No matter how innocent one may be, guilt automatically attaches itself to malicious accusations and cannot help but damage the credibility of the one accused. Rarely are circumstances so clear or situations so simple as to allow the clarification or explanation required to exonerate anyone completely, once the mud has been slung. Guilt of some kind is imputed, whether appropriate or not.

Accusations, whether true or false or somewhere in between, stain one's life. They imprint a blot not soon or easily removed. That is why accusations are so devastating, why hurling them is one of the most malicious things people do to one another.

What is worse is that our corrupt human nature, so prone to sensationalistic titillation, causes us to focus more readily on the accused than on the accuser. There is no such thing in real life as "innocent until proven guilty." Perhaps it is our inner sense of imperfection, our deep though not-often-conscious awareness of our own guilt, that drives us to latch on so quickly to the possible guilt of another. By projecting our own guilt onto others, we attempt to exorcize it from our own conscience, oblivious to the fact that we can never succeed.

For finally, the only way to be free from our guilt is to own it, to recognize and confess our own wrongdoing. Consider this biblical insight:

> They have all gone astray, they are all alike corrupt;
> there is none that does good,
> no, not one.
>
> Psalm 14:3

Only as we confront our own guilt can we be delivered from it. Only then can we truly learn to accept ourselves and one another.

Meanwhile, to be wrongly accused is to learn a peculiar pain in living, a pain made worse when those who accuse us are those for whom we have cared. With bitter sadness the psalmist remembers how, when the people experienced times of trouble, the psalmist sympathized and lent support:

But I, when they were sick . . .
    . . . prayed with head bowed on my bosom,
as though I grieved for my friend or my brother.

Psalm 35:13a, 14a

At some point, they shared in a social contract. They belonged to a common community in which support was mutually given.

But now the community is broken. The connections have been severed, and damage has been done that may prove irreversible. In the end, the accusations wound not only individuals but the whole community. They close doors on the possibility of constructive engagement and reconciliation. Always, out of accusation comes destruction. Even the accuser is diminished by the anger and hostility born within. It is a situation in which no one gains.

Vindication

Vindicate me, O LORD, my God. . . .
Let those who desire my vindication . . .
    be glad. . . .
Then my tongue shall tell of thy righteousness.

Psalm 35:24a, 27a, 28a

To be vindicated is to be released from unjustified criticism and suspicion, to have one's name cleared, to be freed from the oppression of false accusations. To be vindicated is to be absolved from the allegations that have eaten away at one's life like a cancer on the soul.

Deep in our hearts do we not all long to be vindicated, to be set free from the sins that pursue us? For even when we are cleared of external charges, there are still the ones inside that perhaps only we can name. Some of them no one can name. They exist only as a vague, disturbing awareness of our own fallibility, which in turn gives rise to a hunger for real absolution and freedom.

Intrinsic to our longing for release is a desire that it be public, that our innocence—or at least absolution—be witnessed by others. As in community we are accused, so in community do we seek to be freed.

In that sense, vindication is profoundly a product of relationship. It is because we are connected to and derive so much of our self-worth from others that it is to others we turn to have it restored. Others are important for the healing of our wounds because others are so deeply a part of who we are in the first place. Just as our relationships in community are what make accusations threatening, so also our relationships make vindication meaningful. Therefore, our appeal is always external.

In the case of the psalmist the appeal is to God. God, for the psalmist, stands out as the most objective, trustworthy, and knowledgeable witness available. "Thou hast seen, O Lord," the psalmist cries. "Be not silent!" (Ps 35:22). Here, the psalmist, as the one who knows the truth, invokes God's testimony. To believe that there is a vindicating truth is itself a hope and a comfort. But the truth alone may not be enough.

> O LORD, be not far from me!
> Bestir thyself, and awake for my right.
>
> Psalm 35:22, 23a

The psalmist also seeks God's assistance and assurance in recovering from this conflict.

Perhaps the psalmist is aware that while the truth may be liberating, it can also be incriminating. What is needed as much as truth is the presence of one who knows the facts, good and bad, and who is committed to standing alongside us, whatever the facts may be.

At least the psalmist has faith in one to whom to appeal. For many people there is no such recourse. True, God is often the appeal of last resort for believer, partial believer, and unbeliever alike. But in practical experience many people are left with no real sense of support, assurance, or assistance in times of crisis.

Perhaps, like the psalmist, they are fortunate enough to have another advantage. Apparently there were those who stood on the psalmist's side and cared about the outcome—those "who desire my vindication."

In times of trial nothing compares to the presence of supporters. Without any, even victory is hollow. But with supporters, defeat itself becomes bearable. Clearly, when conflict arises, it is crucial to identify, at least for our own peace and encouragement, who it is that might "desire our vindication." Such people are to be treasured and celebrated.

The psalmist's desire that those who showed support share in the joy of vindication may have been quite genuine. Certainly it is natural and even noble to wish happiness and satisfaction for those who stand with us through difficult times. But there is a hint here of bargaining, of suggesting to God that if vindication is given, there will be that many more people stroking God's ego with praise. The psalmist, too, offers to give testimony and praise in return for a successful outcome.

Whether the psalmist meant it that way or not, it is true that one stage of crisis is deal-making. We try to negotiate our way out of trouble with anyone we think can help us, not least of all, God. Plea bargaining is probably as old as our concept of divinity itself.

But it doesn't always work. God is not the cosmic slot machine we wish for. No matter how many tokens of praise or promise we insert, there are no odds that guarantee a tilt toward an eventual jackpot.

Instead we are left with a much more dynamic situation. Grace may come to us in the ways we desire, it may not come at all in immediately apparent terms, or it may surprise us in totally unexpected ways.

Whatever happens, we will be accountable for keeping our side of the bargain in the deals we have made—something few of us are likely to do. In the end, the trials that result from failed promises may prove worse than the trials that gave birth to the promises in the first place. It may be human nature to get into the bargain-making business, but it is a risky business at best.

Our best hope, surely, is vindication based on a higher principle—on a grace that transcends not only our own innocence or guilt but also that of our enemies. For in the end vindication premised on fallible human beings will always be too small.

> Vindicate me, O LORD, my God,
>   according to thy righteousness.

Psalm 35:24

13

Whetted Tongues

Hear my voice, O God, in my complaint;
preserve my life from dread of the enemy,
hide me from the secret plots of the wicked,
from the scheming of evildoers,
who whet their tongues like swords,
who aim bitter words like arrows,
shooting from ambush at the blameless,
shooting at one suddenly and without fear.

Psalm 64:1–4

Some people thrive on gossip. It is a cheap way of building themselves up by tearing others down. Gossip is contemptible, even sad. For what can be so lacking in someone's life that he or she must make up for it through destructive or sensationalistic conversation about others? How unfortunate that there is such a void in some people's lives! That they must fix on someone else's life to give substance to their own! How sad that someone's sense of self-worth is so deficient!

We have all been guilty of gossip at one time or another. Out of frustration with our failures or dissatisfaction with our lives, we unload onto others the criticism that we ourselves deserve but fear. We may also use gossip as an attempt to establish control over others due to a deep sense of personal powerlessness on our part.

Sometimes, the motive for gossip can simply be caring gone wrong. In sharing private information about others, we may mean to express concern, solicit support, or enlist a second opinion. But our efforts may create something entirely new and destructive.

An eighteenth-century philosopher, the Marquis deVauvenargues, put it succinctly: "The usual excuse of those who cause others trouble is that they wish them well."*

For the psalmist, however, the slander was intended. There is no doubt that this was a deliberate attack by people who meant to cause harm. That is one of the nastier possibilities of gossip: By taking shots at others behind their backs, by "shooting from ambush at the blameless" with "bitter words like arrows," we evade responsibility for the damage done. Gossip is hard to prove: It is hard to prove who started it; it is hard to prove it wrong. That is the beauty of gossip. It is such a user-friendly weapon.

Balance

However, the psalmist holds out images of accountability. First, the act of slander is recorded. By naming it we begin to identify the evil for what it is. But more than this, the psalmist pictures a universe where evil is requited, where retribution is meted out in direct proportion to harm done:

> But God will shoot divine arrows at them;
>   they will be wounded suddenly.
> Because of their tongue God will bring them to ruin;
> all who see them will wag their heads.
> Then all people will fear;
>   they will tell what God has wrought,
>   and ponder what God has done.
>
> Psalm 64:7–9

The psalmist may be optimistic. Life hardly seems that balanced or fair most of the time. Still, the image of God shooting back at those who inflict words of injury is not only colorful but encouraging. It appeals to our sense of fairness.

*Quoted in John Baillie, *A Diary of Readings* (New York: Macmillan Publishing Company, 1955).

Somewhere inside us we have a natural sense of balance, a conviction that good should be rewarded and evil undone. Where did we get that idea? Why do we ache to see injuries requited? How did we get this notion of fairness that envisions punishment for slanderous words and destructive deeds? Wherever it comes from, it holds much power.

In the case of this psalm, it is again an issue related to community. For it is not enough that gossip is stopped, wounds healed, and slanderers punished. Fairness calls for a public rendering of justice, a social recognition of the harm done and the punishment meted out.

There is again both a divine and a public court to which the aggrieved appeals. Again there is an image of praise and, in the end, an affirmation of the value of a clean character:

> Let the righteous rejoice in the LORD,
>   and take refuge in [God]!
> Let all the upright in heart glory!
>
> Psalm 64:10

Do we not all need a place of refuge from our accusers, a court of appeal and a protecting cover when the accusing arrows start to fly? Do we not also need to be reassured that there is value in uprightness? For even when we have failed to achieve it ourselves, the ideal of a just standard of behavior provides us with order and meaning. It gives guidance for human relating, and it offers a standard against which to measure ourselves for worse and for better.

People will surely continue to shoot words like arrows into our lives. No doubt we will shoot a few of our own. What takes us beyond them are images of eventual balance or retribution and of better ways to relate in the first place. The former is largely impersonal, though it gives encouragement for the long haul. But with the latter we gain an immediate, personal stake. For as the psalm puts it, the upright in heart can glory in the present. They have the satisfaction of a free conscience, no matter where the arrows are flying.

14

Traps and Snares

Guard me, O LORD, from the hands of the wicked;
  preserve me from violent [people],
  who have planned to trip up my feet.
Arrogant [people] have hidden a trap for me,
  and with cords they have spread a net,
  by the wayside they have set snares for me.

Psalm 140:4-5

Keep me from the trap which they have laid for me,
  and from the snares of evildoers!
Let the wicked together fall into their own nets,
  while I escape.

Psalm 141:9-10

Life is full of traps. There are the ones we set for ourselves and the ones set for us by others. Usually they are hidden. By nature traps are meant to catch us unawares. Indeed, their effectiveness derives from the fact that they catch us in the marginal areas of our lives where we least expect them.

Traps teach us the power of the periphery. They reveal to us our weak points and vulnerabilities. They may reveal unresolved issues in the subconscious that pop up to push us off balance. And despite the fact that our traps lie in the corners and waysides of our lives, they have the power to pull us off the main road and, for a time at least, to disrupt the entire journey.

No wonder the psalmist fears them and asks for help in guarding against them! The psalmist recognizes how valuable it can be to have help in finding where the snares in life might lie. For seldom can we see them all by ourselves. To enlist the help of one who can point out the pitfalls is a wise precaution indeed.

Still, even with the best resources we are likely to hit a few snags, to get tangled in webs of our own making—or of someone else's. It is a miserable feeling. As soon as our foot slips into the net, we begin to lose our freedom. People and circumstances beyond our control gain the upper hand over at least part of our lives. To be trapped is to lose a portion of our autonomy and therefore of ourself.

When we are trapped we often become disoriented, losing sight of our options. Our judgment becomes clouded; our ability to make good choices, short-circuited. We usually have more possibilities than we may discern, but our ability to understand that is distorted.

Being trapped is a frightening experience. Like a wild animal that chews off its foot to get free, we are willing to risk injury to ourselves, our families, or our careers in our struggle to escape. The trap becomes the dominant reality; we cannot see beyond it. In our panic and pain we crash against the enclosing walls, struggling for any way out.

Traps can be suffocating. They squeeze the joy out of life. They choke the spirit and constrict the soul. Sometimes the pressure builds up to where we feel we will burst or go crazy. Our frustration is made worse if we are surrounded by people—however well-meaning—whose agenda is set by the trap itself, so that every move we make and every word we speak is held in suspicion, judged, and used against us. When the psalmist prays, "Preserve me from violent people," the psalmist identifies a fundamental characteristic of traps and of those who oversee them: By nature they are all violent.

But why are there traps in the first place? Where do they come from? Is it not a sad and terrible thought that traps are of human making? That people will actually plan with deliberate malice how to undo one another? What does that say about us? What kind of people are we who would expend such destructive energy with the explicit intention of undermining or damaging another person's life?

Something must have gone dreadfully wrong with our inner matrix, our life-oriented instincts. Our appreciation of community must be seriously flawed, our selfish interests grown way out of proportion, when they lead us to envision gain or, worse yet, to be gratified, by causing the stumbling of another.

Fallen

This is the Fall story of Genesis told over again with a painful new twist. This time the beguiling serpent wears a human face. The undoing of the human community, the corruption of human relationships, and the loss of original peace is the product of the seducing spirit found within humans themselves. We have met the Snake, and he is us.

What makes us so devious that we would seek to tempt, trap, or trip up one another? Is it our own sense of our own insignificance that drives us to raise ourselves up by tearing others down? Is it an attempt to manipulate others to cover our own sense of power-lessness? Are we so threatened by life and each other and, most of all, by the unknown forces within us that we try to assert our-selves by entrapping others? Or are there darker sides to the human personality—greed, lust for power, malice, or a purely sadistic delight in the suffering of others—that account for our facility in setting snares? Whatever the cause, the psalmist's desire to avoid or be delivered from the encircling traps makes sense. May we be delivered even from the desire to set them.

To be wholly delivered, however, we must face another aspect of traps: While some are deliberately, maliciously set by enemies, others ensnare us by the self-destructive tendencies already present within us. These traps are downright attractive. Whether the bait is material, sexual, chemical, or power-oriented, what traps us is our own desire.

To some extent, each of us knows how thoroughly entangled we can get in such snares. We may also have discovered that get-ting out of them can require a great deal of time, pain, patience, and persistence. Perhaps it is because we have set enough snares for ourselves that we react so vehemently to the thought of having our nets multiplied by the snares of others.

In the end, however, the psalmist maintains an image of escape, a vision of deliverance. More than that, there is a wish that the traps would catch those who lay them out in the first place. That's a common sentiment with which we can identify. But better than that would be for us all to be released not only from the traps of our own making and from those made by others but from the kind of enmity and insecurity that motivates traps in the first place.

15

The Judas and Peter Motif

It is not an enemy who taunts me—
then I could bear it; . . .
But it is you, my equal,
my companion, my familiar friend.
We used to hold sweet converse together;
within God's house we walked in fellowship. . . .
My companion stretched out his hand against his friends,
he violated his covenant.
His speech was smoother than butter,
yet war was in his heart;
his words were softer than oil,
yet they were drawn swords.
But thou, O God, wilt cast them down
into the lowest pit.

Psalm 55:12a, 13-14a, 20-21, 23a

What is more bitter than to be betrayed by a friend? It is one thing to suffer the treachery of people who do not pretend to be close to us. But when someone in whom we have trusted turns against us, a deep hole is seared in the soul. Nothing hurts in quite the same way. When we have shared deep pieces of ourselves, entrusting, as it were, a portion of our own being into another's keeping, it becomes almost unbearable that such trust should be violated and abused. Betrayal is a particularly humiliating and intensely personal kind of offense. It is a rape of the soul.

Betrayal is possible only between friends. Enemies cannot betray each other; they are already alienated. Betrayal is distinctly a function of having been in a trust relationship in the first place. The deeper the trust, the more potent are the possibilities for betrayal.

In a sense, friendship is the flip side of betrayal. It is a declaration of connectedness in a world that knows alienation too well. To trust another person is to fling a gauntlet in the face of betrayal, to believe that commitment, love, and loyalty will prove stronger than the temptation to act unfaithfully toward the other.

Our optimism is often premature. We human beings are far too fallible to maintain all of our trusts intact. Almost inevitably, we will fail at some of them.

Because friendship and betrayal are so powerfully related, the bitterness that comes from a broken trust is doubly strong. In fact, most of the time our pain at betrayal issues forth in a consuming anger, as we see in the psalmist's case:

> Let death come upon them;
> let them go down to Sheol alive;
> let them go away in terror to their graves.
>
> Psalm 55:15

Betrayal hurts so deeply because it involves such great loss. Even when it stems from an effort by those who love us to confront us with hard realities that need to be faced, still there is a sense of trust betrayed. We must mourn the loss of relationships that may never be the same. Sometimes confrontation brings healing and a greater trust than existed before. But in many cases it means the total loss of relationships that cannot be redeemed.

At a deeper level there is another, more disturbing kind of loss. When trusts are betrayed, we lose confidence in our ability to discern who is trustworthy and who is not. We begin to doubt our own judgment. If we have once made a life-damaging mistake in investing our trust, how can we know that we will not do so again? Our confidence is undermined, sometimes to the point where we become afraid to trust anyone.

But to never trust again is a tragedy greater than having lost trust in the first place. That leaves us in a most lonely, most unhealthy isolation. Trust broken is a bitter experience, but it is not the end of our possibilities for relationship. If we do not trust again, we diminish ourselves. For trust, as it bonds us to others, is necessary for our growth and healing. Through trust, we ground our being in a reality greater than ourselves.

Never will there be guarantees that our trusts will not be broken. Our decision to trust again may be better informed, but we can never know the outcome of our choices in advance. To trust requires that we take an almost divine kind of risk—for God, according to Scripture, takes such a risk with us. None of us is perfect enough to merit absolute trust. Yet there is something about being trusted that itself can give us the will to be worthy of the faith placed in us. Trust, in that sense, is one of our noblest human capacities.

Origins

But we are still left with the possibility and the pain of trusts broken. The reality of betrayal remains. Certainly, where betrayals have already poisoned our lives, we must come to terms with our experience. Otherwise we can be consumed by anger and resentment for years, victimized over and over again, not so much by enemies but by our own unresolved sorrow and pain.

One way to move beyond resentment is to examine why people betray each other in the first place. Quite easily we can discern such factors as greed, jealousy, fear, weakness, and self-preservation. But seldom will we be able to fully understand what motivates one person to betray the trust of another. Generally, a complex blend of internal and external pressures accumulate to the point that self-interest overrides loyalty to one's friend or loved one. Or, a person may become unable to discern any more what constitutes either aid or betrayal to a friend. Sometimes the mere fact that a person has never experienced being fully loved or trusted may cause that person to play out his or her sense of being untrustworthy by actually proving to be so. We humans are amazingly complex creatures, often, tragically so.

But there is another way of understanding where betrayal comes from. That is by facing the betrayer within, the Peter and Judas within us.

Historians and scholars have never fully agreed on what motivated Judas in the story of Jesus' betrayal. Nor are we certain what went through Peter's mind on the night he denied his Master three times. We do know that both men suffered profound remorse and deep agony of spirit when they realized what they had done. Judas was so grieved that he could no longer bear to live. He publicly repudiated his deed and then committed an ugly suicide.

Peter, however, perhaps lacking Judas' conscience and courage, retreated into self-pity. Yet it was Peter who was chosen to lead Jesus' disciples. Is it not symbolic that a man who had failed so utterly should not only be redeemed by a grace totally outside himself but placed in a position of authority? Is that not a spectacular lesson to us that no failure is unredeemable? For if Peter, who denied his very Savior at his most critical hour of need, could be redeemed, restored, and trusted again, what does that say about the new possibilities for us?

Perhaps Peter didn't realize what he was doing when he betrayed the one he loved most. Nor perhaps did Judas foresee the consequences of the events he set in motion. So often, that is how betrayal works. People don't realize what they're doing. Peter and Judas may both have thought they were doing Jesus a favor, trying to position themselves or influence circumstances for an outcome that in their distorted vision they saw as constructive.

How often do we do the same? In our ignorance, shortsightedness, and presumption, do we not frequently risk sending someone to a cross through our own misguided judgments? It is a possibility to ponder.

But so is Peter's redemption. Peter and Judas represent two possibilities for each of us. On the one hand, our failures and betrayals can destroy us, as in Judas' case. They can make life unbearable. On the other hand, we may be touched by a grace that not only heals and restores us but works through our woundedness for the good of others, as happened with Peter.

Yet the story of Peter's failure remains, and it mitigates against any self-righteousness on the part of the one restored. We all need to live in the knowledge that Peter the denier and Judas the betrayer live within us all.

Our consolation lies in words like those of the Last Supper, that most central act of Christian worship, the most holy moment of which begins with the words, "On the night in which he was *betrayed*. . . ." For there we come to face fully both our own fallibility and the simultaneous possibility of complete forgiveness. In such moments we meet the fantastic possibility of a love that can obliterate our inadequacy and proclaim us whole.

Betrayal may be one of the darkest possibilities of human relationship. But beyond it there is hope that it is not the final act of which we are capable. There is a love that transcends and redeems even betrayal.

16

Curses and Vengeance

May this be the reward of my accusers from the LORD, . . .
Appoint a wicked man against him;
  let an accuser bring him to trial.
When he is tried, let him come forth guilty;
  let his prayer be counted as sin!
May his days be few;
  may another seize his goods!
May his children be fatherless,
  and his wife a widow!
May his children wander about and beg;
  may they be driven out of the ruins they inhabit!
May the creditor seize all that he has;
  may strangers plunder the fruits of his toil!
Let there be none to extend kindness to him,
  nor any to pity his fatherless children!
May his posterity be cut off;
  may his name be blotted out . . .
  and may his memory be cut off from the earth!

                              Psalm 109:20a, 6-13a, 15b

Some of the psalm writers really knew how to curse! When it comes
to wishing evil on an enemy, their vivid invectives make our common curses look puny. Few of us are as bold, as thorough, or as
original as some of the psalm writers in specifying the kind of harm
we might like to see come to our enemies.

That is not to say that we feel any less angry or bitter than they did. We, too, express our anger in hostile thoughts and words. We, too, thirst for revenge or retribution and imagine ways in which that might come to those who have hurt us. Even when our hostilities are private and our animosities unspoken, there is frequently in our hearts a lingering desire to get even.

Seldom, however, do we get as nasty as the psalmist or as gutsy in venting our hostility. We would not dare say today some of the things the psalm writers got away with. Their curses ranged from the common to the chilling. On the milder side we find:

> Let them be put to shame and confused altogether
>   who seek to snatch away my life;
> let them be turned back and brought to dishonor
>   who desire my hurt!
>
> Psalm 40:14

Getting a bit nastier and, in a sense, almost amusing are curses such as, "Make their loins tremble continually" (Ps 69:23b). That is something like wishing an adversary permanent diarrhea!

On the more frightening side, we find this curse: "Let them be blotted out of the book of the living" (Ps 69:28a). This refers not only to present life but to all future existence as well. Its bitter demand is for nothing less than total obliteration—past, present, and future—not only of the person being cursed but of the very memory of that person in the minds of others.

At the most chilling extreme we find such bitter rage as that voiced by the Israelites during their captivity in Babylon. In cursing their enemies, the Israelites cried,

> Happy shall [be the person] who takes your little ones
>   and dashes them against the rock!
>
> Psalm 137:9

Even in our most angry moments, most of us would have a hard time justifying the smashing of little children's heads against rocks, even if they were the children of our foes. Such an act borders more on insanity than on justice.

How, then, shall we understand these colorful curses of our fore-bears? How seriously should we take them? What do they tell us about our own capacity for anger and vengeance? Do they give us permission to articulate equally violent pronouncements in our own day?

It does not take much reflection to recognize where our curses come from. They are the products of our anger, our bruised ego, our need to express the deep hurts we feel. Curses function as an outlet for the powerful emotions aroused in us when we feel wronged. If they serve no other purpose, they put us in touch with how deep and how strong our negative emotions can be. They remind us of that seething ill will that can be birthed and nurtured in the darker regions of the soul, both to our own detriment and to that of others. Perhaps our curses are warning signals of those boundaries beyond which it is not healthy for anger to go.

To that extent, curses and the malicious fantasies that often go with them can actually be useful in focusing and venting our anger before it consumes us or gets channeled into actions as destructive as the desires embodied in the words. Indeed, one reason that curses exist is to be a substitute for action. They describe what we would like to do if we could, as opposed to what we are actually free to do—at least without creating even more destructive results.

That is where God often gets drawn into our curses. We turn to God to do those things to our enemies that we are neither willing nor able to do ourselves. Our appeal for divine justice frequently reflects the reality that justice cannot or will not otherwise be done as we think it should be.

We see that kind of attitude expressed in the opening words of the first passage quoted above. The psalmist appeals for a third party to initiate a trial in which the offender will be found guilty and punished. It is an indication of the passion of the curses that the psalmist wants even the prayers of the accused to be considered sinful. Not an ounce of pity or mercy is present in the psalmist's heart.

Perhaps, then, it is good that we are not usually able to implement judgment on our own terms. By projecting or releasing our controversies into the hands of a greater authority, we find at least some relief from the immediate pressures of our own hostility. Then too, time may prove that justice delayed can sometimes be justice improved. For once tempers have cooled and hindsight has had time to engage, situations that once brought forth curses may be more wisely resolved.

Vengeance

Still, we carry this thirst for revenge. It is not one of our nobler attributes. Nor is revenge biblical, although the desire for it, as expressed in the psalms, is obviously allowed. In fact, Scripture makes a fairly clear distinction between revenge and vengeance. Our modern usage of the words might confuse us here by equating the two, but they are not the same in the biblical view.

In the perspective of the psalmist's day vengeance had a positive rather than a negative connotation. It was to be a process of restoration to wholeness, a returning to proper balance of relationships and events that had gotten out of kilter. To achieve the constructive goals of vengeance, certain prescribed actions for setting things right were developed.

It soon became clear, however, that human nature is much too volatile to be bound by an orderly process of social balancing. Ultimately, only God can be objective and restrained enough to accomplish justice without excess. Consequently, by New Testament times the attitude had developed that the Christians sought to adopt as their own: "Beloved, never avenge yourselves, but leave it to the wrath of God; for it is written, 'Vengeance is mine, I will repay, says the Lord' " (Rom 12:19).

Left to ourselves, we pursue not vengeance but revenge. Our hunger to do as much or more harm to others as we feel has been done to us usually sets off a cycle of violence that only makes matters worse for all concerned.

In the Middle East or Northern Ireland today, for example, we see with painful clarity the product of the human thirst for revenge. There is no orderly restoring of balance and wholeness as intended by the biblical vision of vengeance. Instead, there is a self-perpetuating cycle of destruction. Curses that once were only verbal have now been translated into a devastating physical reality that consumes whole communities and costs innocent lives.

That shows us one of the most frightening aspects of cursing, namely, that the judgments we pronounce may well come back on our own heads. In our spite and hardheartedness, we may end up formulating our own destruction.

One way to keep ourselves in check is to stop and ask, Who might be cursing *us*? What have we done that another might take as injury? By recognizing our own culpability, we are reminded that as justified as our anger may be, none of us is so perfect as to be exempt from judgment ourselves.

In the meantime, we may honestly put our curses into verbal form. We may hurl them against the heavens and invoke divine retribution on our opponents if we please. But in the end, it is better to leave the actual outcome of our pronouncements to a higher power or a greater reality than ourselves.

The very existence of these words of cursing in Scripture gives us permission to express our anger and pain. In these biblical invectives our feelings of frustration and bitterness—that whole side of what it is to be human—are acknowledged and allowed. Such imprecatory psalms, as they are formally called, are often omitted from prayer books and hymnals because they are considered inappropriate for enlightened believers. But it may also be grace that from time to time we can reclaim these emotive old words and utilize them constructively in our moments of pain.

17

Innocence and Justice

O LORD my God, in thee do I take refuge;
  save me from all my pursuers, and deliver me,
lest like a lion they rend me,
  dragging me away, with none to rescue.
O LORD my God, if I have done this,
  if there is wrong in my hands,
if I have requited my friend with evil
  or plundered my enemy without cause,
let the enemy pursue me and overtake me,
  and . . . trample my life to the ground,
  and lay my soul in the dust. . . .
The LORD judges the peoples;
  judge me, O LORD, according to my righteousness
  and according to the integrity that is in me.

Psalm 7:1-5a, 8

These are bold words. They are words of both fear and confidence that contain key components for surviving adversity. From these words we can glean insight and encouragement for our own struggles.

First comes the fear. Already in the ominous reference to pursuers we sense the anxiety that underlies the psalm. Clearly, forces that threaten the future are at work. Almost by definition, to be pursued means to have one's security put at risk. When one is pursued, an element of uncertainty is introduced, and with it, a growing sense of pressure.

The psalmist expands this picture of anxiety by connecting it with the image of a lion waiting to pounce upon and dismember its victim. In this vivid image of being torn apart and dragged away there is a frightening reminder of all those forces that can overpower us and shred our fragile spirits. We are, after all, immensely vulnerable people. The idea that there will be no one to rescue us when the lion does come only increases the feeling of helplessness and dread the psalmist tries to convey.

These images represent the real and very ugly possibilities that arise when enemies stalk us. Knowing what harm others can do to us is frightening. Such knowledge often produces a kind of cold, sinking, sickening, even paralyzing feeling inside. Whether we like it or not, we recognize that there are lions in our lives, both internal and external, that can destroy us. We would be foolish not to fear them.

But in the psalmist's case there is a conviction even in the midst of fear that the attack of this lion is unjustified. It is almost as if the psalmist is puzzling to understand why the attack is occurring at all: "*If* I have done this, *if* there is wrong in my hands. . . ."

We understand such wondering. For there are times in our lives when the lions unexpectedly gather with menacing growls, threatening to devour us.

If we are like the psalmist, we may be able to appeal our case and draw in witnesses and an impartial judge for our vindication. But how many of us would actually dare to risk our very lives in the process, as the psalmist does? How many of us would have the courage to bet our souls that the court would rule in our favor?

Obviously, the psalmist is confident that the evidence will prove the attacks unjustified. In fact, the psalmist is not the least bit afraid to invoke the heavenly court and to insist that the judgment be issued publicly:

> Arise, O LORD, in thy anger,
>   lift thyself up against the fury of my enemies. . . .
> Let the assembly of the peoples be gathered about thee;
>   and over it take thy seat on high.
>
> Psalm 7:6a, 7

There is a sense of righteous indignation in the psalmist's tone—not uncommon in our own response to being accused. The only question is whether our indignation is *self*-righteous, whether it is based on our own self-serving criteria of justice or on a higher standard. For self-righteous indignation will only increase our danger.

Presuppositions

Beyond who's right and who's wrong in the psalmist's account lies a deeper truth. There are some presuppositions about life and justice that make the whole enterprise meaningful. Underlying the psalm is a belief that justice exists, that appeals for it are sensible because there is order and meaning to life. In face, this psalm portrays a very ordered picture of the universe.

There are, first, norms by which the psalmist's complaint can be measured, though these are assumed here and not all laid out. Then there is an image of a court of appeal, both human and divine, reigned over by an ultimate Referee who is by nature wholly just and impartial.

Throughout the psalm there is a deep trust in God as one who has the power to limit and rectify injustice and to promote that which is good:

> O let the evil of the wicked come to an end,
>   but establish thou the righteous,
> thou who triest the minds and hearts,
>   thou righteous God. . . .
> God is a righteous judge,
>   and a God who has indignation every day.
>
> Psalm 7:9, 11

Presupposed, too, in this ordered view of the universe, is the typical Old Testament belief that ultimately evil will be punished and good rewarded. At times, in fact, the psalms portray an almost karmic view of rewards and punishments. In this psalm the writer simply declares:

Behold, the wicked man conceives evil,
and is pregnant with mischief,
and brings forth lies.
He makes a pit, digging it out,
and falls into the hole which he has made.
His mischief returns upon his own head,
and on his own pate his violence descends.

Psalm 7:14-16

Early in the development of Hebrew thought there was no concept of heaven as we understand it today. That is why justice had to be meted out in this lifetime. There was no expected afterlife in which people would be punished for their sins. But as time went on, it became painfully clear that justice is all too often not done at all in this lifetime, that the scales do not end up balanced, that indeed the wicked often prosper. Some people have argued that this fundamental awareness of the unfairness and imbalance of life is one reason why heaven became necessary. The concept of an afterlife offers the possibility of good being rewarded and evil punished. What is left unresolved in this lifetime is settled in the next.

Be that as it may, the fact remains that what enables the psalmist to find comfort and hope in this situation of conflict, what can support and encourage us as well, is a confidence in the fundamental ordered-ness of life. Either consciously or unconsciously we all need and hold to some world-view, some set of standards, by which life becomes sensible. Without an ideal of balance, without a belief in accountability, life becomes unmanageable. Without the conviction that behavior may be either responsible or irresponsible as determined by agreed-upon norms in a given social context, there is no hope for social cohesion or individual security. To cope with conflict we need faith in a potentially positive outcome.

Value and Thankfulness

At a deeper level, the existence of social norms and the belief in an ordered universe tie in with our sense of personal value. It is because the psalmist had a sense of self-worth that it mattered whether he was innocent or guilty. Such a sense of self-worth may itself be testimony to the ordered, meaningful universe in which we battle against our lions and appeal for justification.

Based on the conviction that righteousness will ultimately prevail, the psalmist offers thanks and praise as the appropriate response to deliverance and the enactment of justice. Such a response reflects a valuing of the self who is saved. It also suggests that praise and thanksgiving are necessary components of a properly ordered universe.

> I will give to the LORD
>> the thanks due to God's righteousness,
>> and I will sing praise to the name
>> of the LORD, the Most High.

Psalm 7:17

18

Trampled Times

Be gracious to me, O God,
  for adversaries trample upon me;
  all day long foes oppress me;
my enemies trample upon me all day long. . . .
All day long they seek to injure my cause;
  all their thoughts are against me for evil. . . .
Thou hast kept count of my tossings;
  put thou my tears in thy bottle!
  Are they not in thy book?
Then my enemies will be turned back
  in the day when I call.
  This I know, that God is for me. . . .
in God I trust without a fear.
  What can [others] do to me?

Psalm 56:1, 2a, 5, 8-9, 11

This psalm is a product of the trampled times. We all have those times when the pressure gets to us, when the struggle gets us down. In the trampled times we feel exhausted, defeated, run down, oppressed. The trampled times are times of a deep and heavy sadness.

Like a broken record, we repeat ourselves. Our emotional resources become so depleted we cannot see beyond the immediate cycle of oppression. The mind clouds over, and we become preoccupied with the threats against us. Like the psalmist, we cannot seem to stop focusing on whatever is oppressing us. It is as though we cannot believe it's real. By turning it over again and again in our minds, we hope to comprehend what has happened and to discern some way out. Sometimes we are simply amazed, and we wonder how we got into such a situation in the first place.

The trampled times are down times. They are depressed times, times we feel dumped on. During the trampled times a lot of life gets squeezed out of us. Our energy is drained. For us as for the psalmist, these trampled times seem relentless.

> All day long [foes] oppress me;
> my enemies trample upon me all day long.
>
> Psalm 56:1b, 2a

It would be enough if only portions of our day were preoccupied with our problems. But sometimes the pressure just doesn't let up. It feels as though every waking moment—and some of our sleeping ones as well—are dominated by the oppression we feel. We can understand the psalmist's prayer, "Be gracious to me, O God." For during the trampled times we need somebody somewhere to be gracious to us. If nobody close by will be gracious, we can only hope that God will.

During the down times it's easy to get paranoid. We often see things as worse than they are, and that in turn drags us down further. Our perceptions can be affected both by our suffering and by the self-pity or sorrow that often follows.

Then too, we are weaker during the trampled times. Events and accusations that would not normally disturb us grow out of proportion when we are vulnerable, confused, or emotionally confined to a shorter range of options. The scale of stability changes. On the new scale the forces against us loom larger and more dangerous than they otherwise would. When we are vulnerable, it takes less to hurt us.

Recovery

Trampled times are bottom times. They reduce us emotionally, physically, and mentally. At the bottom we may come to a deep emptiness, an impenetrable darkness, or to towering walls beyond which we cannot see. But another possibility of the bottom is that because we have been there and survived, we know of new resources and new capacities within ourselves. Sometimes the mere fact that we have survived great assaults is substantial enough assurance to keep us going and to help us see beyond the present gloom. Indeed, the human capacity for survival is remarkable.

Sometimes we can become quite feisty at the bottom. For one thing there is little left to lose, or so it may seem. Remaining traces of anger may still cause us to spit and fume. So may a bitter nihilism—an "I don't give a damn anymore" attitude. But on the positive side, both of these may keep us going, at least for a while.

At the bottom we may discover new aspects of our character that can help us endure and grow. A sense of humor may reemerge to help us survive by casting our difficult circumstances into different perspectives. Then, too, there are times at the bottom when we connect with powerful external resources that can give us the courage to persevere.

Perhaps all of these elements are involved in the psalmist's cry:

> What can flesh do to me? . . .
> In God I trust without a fear.
> What can [others] do to me?
>
> Psalm 56:4b, 11

Obviously, "flesh" and "others" have done plenty to the psalmist, which is why this psalm exists in the first place. But the psalmist also has a firm sense of something beyond the current reality, of a portion of life that cannot be touched or destroyed by opposition.

Is this simply a way to inject hope into a dismal situation? Is it escapism or wishful thinking? Or is it an enlightened, healthy attitude that transcends a seemingly no-win situation?

The psalmist clearly has no doubt that hope is justified. Indeed, the psalmist moves far beyond hope to a confident declaration of self-worth based on the value of a relationship with God in which the self finds meaning and affirmation. There is, in fact, a remarkable intimacy in the way the psalmist describes God's interest in personal suffering:

> Thou hast kept count of my tossings;
> Put thou my tears in thy bottle!
> Are they not in thy book?

Psalm 56:8

In this image of God there is a belief that nothing is lost, that every ounce of our personal suffering is recorded. Is it not a profound and comforting thought to imagine that every tear we shed, every pain we suffer, is noticed? Our suffering is known! What more could we wish for in our desire for comfort and eventual justice? This is a picture of a wholistic universe, a totally integrated cosmos where the divine awareness absorbs even our silent sorrows.

In such a world we can never be defeated simply by the machinations of enemies, no matter how wicked or how successful they may be in the short run. Eternity is on our side in such a cosmos. It becomes true that no one can ultimately prevail over us. For in the breadth and memory and compassion of the divine mind our sufferings are not only noticed but recompensed: "Then my enemies will be turned back . . ." (Ps 56:9a).

Response

Again, in this psalm, the writer relates deliverance to thanksgiving. The psalmist defines the saving relationship as one that includes a mutual commitment: "My vows to thee I must perform, O God" (Ps 56:12a), and one that culminates in thanksgiving and praise: "I will render thank offerings to thee" (Ps 56:12b).

We, too, need an attitude of gratefulness and self-giving in order to find a healthy balance in life. Without commitments to draw us out of ourselves, we cannot fully develop. Only by living in mutually demanding relationships can we establish our most positive identities and cultivate our best capacities.

In such relationships gratitude demonstrates a proper sense of self-perspective. It shows that we understand the limits of our own being and the value of others. It is a sign of the connectedness without which we would fail to achieve meaningful being.

The outcome of all this is summarized by the psalmist in a lovely vision of new possibilities. Beyond the trampled times, beyond the tears and despite the suffering caused by those who conspire against us, there is the dream of a bright new way to live. We don't have to remain at the bottom.

> For thou hast delivered my soul from death,
>   yea, my feet from falling,
> that I may walk before God
>   in the light of life.

Psalm 56:13

19

Betrayal and Revenge

As for me, I said, "O LORD, be gracious to me;
heal me, for I have sinned against thee!"
My enemies say of me in malice:
"When will he die, and his name perish?" . . .
All who hate me whisper together about me;
they imagine the worst for me.
Even my bosom friend in whom I trusted,
who ate of my bread, has [betrayed me].
But do thou, O LORD, be gracious to me,
and raise me up, that I may requite them!
By this I know that thou are pleased with me,
in that my enemy has not triumphed over me.

Psalm 41:4-5, 7, 9-11

There is an odd turn in the progression of this psalm, which begins not with the words above but with a statement about how
God will be gracious to those who care for the weak and the
troubled:

Blessed [are those] who consider the [weak]!
The LORD delivers [them] in the day of trouble.

Psalm 41:1

Within four verses, however, the writer switches gears. All of
a sudden there is no more mention of the weak. Instead, there is
a bitter diatribe against the psalmist's enemies. In addition, no one

has proved to be caring or helpful during the psalmist's own time of need. Instead of receiving comfort and aid, the psalmist feels abandoned and betrayed. People who had been friends have suddenly changed their loyalties:

> And when [people come] to see me,
>   [they utter] empty words,
>   while [their hearts gather] mischief.
>
> Psalm 41:6

Isn't it depressing how quickly people can turn against each other? Unquestionably, one of life's bitterest lessons is finding out how easily acquaintances can turn into adversaries. Sometimes their motives are transparent. They see an opportunity for personal gain. They get caught up in the sensationalism of the moment. Or they are afraid of getting tainted themselves by the suffering of another. But sometimes these betrayals are simply sad reflections of how fickle humans can be.

That is not to say that we are all bad or incapable of loyalty in the midst of adversity. On the contrary, some of the most uplifting examples of friendship come during times of great crisis. Whether it's because of a story we hear on the news or through personal experience, we are sometimes moved to amazement by the incredible generosity and caring that people can show even for complete strangers in times of need.

But on those occasions when our sufferings are self-induced and not the product of some accident or natural disaster, when we transgress against the established public norms, then we discover the real nature of the commitments of those we call friends. Finding out who our friends really are is both one of the best and one of the most disappointing discoveries in life. Times of crisis usually reveal both.

In this case the psalmist acknowledges personal failure. His or her actions are admitted as sin, as a violation of acceptable norms. But then the psalmist goes on to imply that the actions of others are just as bad or worse. The reactions to the psalmist's trouble produce added suffering, presumably out of all proportion to the initial wrong. Instead of sympathy and support, there is gossip, collusion, and resentment. Who are these "friends" anyway, to be so two-faced and judgmental?

Perhaps the psalmist is being mean spirited. Could the psalmist simply be whining? Or are the complaints justified? We will never know. But we do know from our own experience how unpleasant it is when people offer fake sympathy yet actually delight in our distress. No matter what the circumstances, the thought that other people actually wish us ill is depressing.

Worst of all is the betrayal of a close friend, one whom we have trusted more intimately than others. Few experiences in life are as bitter or produce such deep pain. However, these relationships, when mended, often produce a deeper bond than existed before. Unfortunately, mending isn't always possible. The pain and estrangement can grow too deep. Such, apparently, was the psalmist's situation. For instead of reconciliation, the psalmist prays for revenge: "raise me up, that I might requite them!" (Ps 41:10b).

The desire for revenge is a part of our human nature. In Old Testament thought, however, there is a move away from leaving revenge in human hands. Instead there is vengeance, understood to be a positive restoration of balance and something to be left to God, who alone can discern the whole truth and administer appropriate justice.

Retribution

Various psalms convey the Hebrew conviction that there will in the end be a balance for every person, a settling of accounts for rights and wrongs. Two such passages illustrate this view:

> Take me not off with the wicked,
>   with those who are workers of evil. . . .
> Requite them according to their work,
>   and according to the evil of their deeds;
> requite them according to the work of their hands;
>   render them their due reward.
>
> Psalm 28:3a, 4

> For thou dost requite [us]
> according to [our] work.
>
> Psalm 62:12b

In each case the assumption is that the scales will one day be balanced. A higher reality than that in which we now live will bring appropriate compensation to us all.

By New Testament times this view becomes more fully mature. There we find not only a full-blown concept of heaven and hell, where good and bad are rewarded accordingly, but also such radical words as those of Jesus, himself a Jewish rabbi and child of the Old Testament, who says, "Love your enemies, do good to those who hate you, bless those who curse you, pray for those who abuse you" (Luke 6:27-8).

These words are almost beyond our capacity to comprehend, much less to obey. Something deep within us rebels at the thought of our adversaries going unpunished for their misdeeds.

Yet these words contain a profound vision of human potential as well as very practical advice for coping with life's inequities. To be able to let go of animosity toward our enemies is extraordinarily difficult under the best of circumstances. But not to do so can injure us further, for it takes a great deal of energy to carry grudges. Psychologically, we need to let go of our anger and resentment in order to find healing. Up to a certain point, the anger may indeed be part of the healing process. Beyond that point, the effort we put into perpetuating our hostility diminishes our spirit and delays our recovery.

By seeking to implement Jesus' advice and by drawing upon whatever resources of grace we need to do that—prayer, counseling, confession, community support—we can more quickly be freed from those lingering forces of hostility that consume so much energy. Adopting this radically different attitude toward our enemies can help us cool down until we learn to let go of the animosity, before it drains us.

Heaven

At the same time, to forgive one's enemies is to create a new kind of positive energy in the universe, a foretaste of what "heaven" symbolizes. Indeed, one vision of heaven is of a place where we are so overwhelmed by the grace of being released from our own imperfections that the hostility we carry toward others becomes easy to release. Seen in this perspective, our faults and the faults of others, even those of our enemies, become trivial. Once we have been energized by that eternal grace, we become empowered to exercise more grace in our own lives. It may not be a quality that comes naturally. But it is one of those points of transcendence where we are able to rise to a higher level.

Obviously, the psalm writer wasn't there yet or perhaps not even headed in that direction. For this psalm writer as for others of that age, salvation was defined by one's relation to one's enemy.

> By this I know that thou are pleased with me,
> in that my enemy has not triumphed over me.
>
> Psalm 41:11

Elsewhere in the psalms we find similar statments:

> For thou hast delivered me from every trouble,
> and my eye has looked in triumph on my enemies.
>
> Psalm 54:7

> And now my head shall be lifted up
> above my enemies round about me.
>
> Psalm 27:6

> [They are] called blessed in the land;
> thou dost not give [them] up to
> the will of [their] enemies.
>
> Psalm 41:2b

These passages and others like them show how powerful enemy imagery was to the psalm writers, how threatened they felt at so many different times, both in their personal and national lives. We today have advantages they lacked. We probably have more physical security. But we also have the wisdom of later ages, which helps us process our feelings about enemies in more constructive ways.

Still, it can be a comfort to know that others have felt as threatened, as hostile, and as hurt as we sometimes do. Perhaps the combination of that knowledge and the accumulated wisdom of later generations can help us become the kind of people the psalmist lauds in the beginning of this psalm, namely, people who show compassion for those who are weak and in need.

20

Confidence

Save me, O God, by thy name,
   and vindicate me by thy might. . . .
For insolent [people] have risen against me,
   ruthless [people] seek my life; . . .
   in thy faithfulness put an end to them.

Psalm 54:1, 3a, 5b

The LORD is my light and my salvation;
   whom shall I fear?
The LORD is the stronghold of my life;
   of whom shall I be afraid?
When evildoers assail me,
   uttering slanders against me,
my adversaries and foes,
   they shall stumble and fall.
Though a host encamp against me,
   my heart shall not fear. . . .
Wait for the LORD;
   be strong, and let your heart take courage;
   yea, wait for the LORD!

Psalm 27:1-3a, 14

The number of psalms about adversity is quite amazing. So many of the psalms are the products of interpersonal conflict. A kind of enemy mentality predominates in which the suffering described is a result of personal attacks and the blessing sought is the destruction of adversaries. A surprisingly strong sense of life being full of conflict pervades these psalms. Accordingly, they reflect the range of emotions that strong conflict engenders: anger, bitterness, fear, anxiety, estrangement, hope.

But in the two selections above a different tone emerges. In each of them the sense of conflict is strong, the dangers disturbing:

> Ruthless [people] seek my life.
>
> Psalm 54:3a

> Give me not up to the will of my adversaries;
> for false witnesses have risen against me,
> and they breathe out violence.
>
> Psalm 27:12

But at the same time, there is a clear confidence in the face of such adversity. There is a calm assurance that the outcome will be in the psalmist's favor, that ultimately the psalmist will survive and be safe.

Part of this confidence may derive from the fact that in both cases, retribution is signed over completely to God. In some previous, perhaps more volatile situations, other psalm writers have clung to the possibility of exercising a portion of retribution themselves. Here the more primitive instinct for revenge has given way to a real trust that accounts will be settled and security restored.

Perhaps the writers of these psalms were further removed from the immediate conflicts. Perhaps when they penned these verses they were less disheartened, more objective, buoyed up by friends, or simply in better spirits.

However, there is no less fear or passion involved here. To one of the writers, the faithfulness requested of God means no less than the utter destruction of the perceived enemies:

> [God] will requite my enemies with evil;
> in thy faithfulnes put an end to them.
>
> Psalm 54:5b

This desire is neither mild nor compassionate.

Nevertheless, there is a sublime assurance in both psalms that deliverance will inevitably come.

> Behold, God is my helper;
>   the Lord is the upholder of my life.
>
> Psalm 54:4

> For [God] will hide me in [a] shelter
>   in the day of trouble;
> [and] will conceal me under the cover of [God's] tent,
>   [God] will set me high upon the rock.
>
> Psalm 27:5

There is a strong sense here not only of guaranteed deliverance but also of safe and secure refuge in times of trouble. Where does the psalmist get this assurance? What accounts for the difference in the perspective between these and other psalms? More important, how can *we* find such confidence?

Perhaps we will never know why in one case the psalm writer is confident and in another case disheartened. We ourselves experience different moods on different days. Our personalities differ. Our faith in ourselves and in a higher power waxes and wanes at different stages in life.

Clearly, the concepts that shape our understanding of reality make a difference. If we believe in the same kind of God as did the psalm writers, we, too, can grow toward that act of faith that allows us to let go of our fears and hostilities. We, too, can trust that not only will justice finally be done but that we will be graciously looked after in the meantime. This was the psalmist's belief, stated explicitly:

> I believe that I shall see the goodness of the LORD
>   in the land of the living!
>
> Psalm 27:13

The psalmist's picture of a hiding place, of a refuge, of being led to a high place removed from the battlefields of life, is appealing. We all long for such breathing space, for such islands of peace in the midst of our struggles. Perhaps, to some degree, we can move closer to the rocks of refuge simply by allowing ourselves to imagine them and letting the vision of such vantage points give us comfort and a sense of hope.

To be sure, it makes a huge difference in our emotional state when we sense that we have the kind of support in which the psalmist trusted. Support structures make an enormous difference in our ability to survive, to recover from crises, and to achieve and maintain a healthy state in general.

Patience

Another key ingredient described so beautifully in Psalm 27 is patience, the ability simply to wait. To wait constructively through times of trial requires great strength and considerable faith. For the psalmist, one of the things that helped was a specific idea of what it was that was waited for. We, too, need to identify what motivates us and offers us hope. That, in turn, can provide us with the beginnings of courage. The kind of courage recommended by the psalmist is a good yardstick for helping us to measure our own attitudes as we face adversity.

Even if we never achieve the psalmist's degree of confidence, we can take courage from the fact that such confidence is possible. After all the accounts of trials and traumas engendered by enemies, it is refreshing to find a model of hope and security. In the midst of a world still fraught with adversity, these images of confidence stand out. They offer us assurance that a positive outcome to our conflicts is possible after all.

> Be strong, and let your heart take courage;
> yea, wait for the LORD!
>
> Psalm 27:14b

21

Innocence

Hear a just cause, O LORD; attend to my cry!
Give ear to my prayer from lips free of deceit! . . .
If thou triest my heart, if thou visitest me by night,
if thou testest me, thou wilt find no wickedness in me;
my mouth does not transgress. . . .
I have avoided the ways of the violent.
My steps have held fast to thy paths,
my feet have not slipped. . . .
Keep me as the apple of thy eye;
hide me in the shadow of thy wings,
from the wicked who despoil me,
my deadly enemies who surround me.

Psalm 17:1, 3, 4b, 5, 8-9

Enter not into judgment with thy servant;
for no [one] living is righteous before thee.

Psalm 143:2

What is innocence? Who can claim it? The psalmist does. In most of the psalms there is an implicit suggestion that the psalmist's troubles are undeserved. The appeals for vindication, the cries for help, and the diatribes against enemies are constructed in such a way as to build our sympathy for the psalmist. We never hear the enemies' side of the story.

Oh, there are times when the psalmist admits wrongdoing, at least in passing.

O God, thou knowest my folly;
  the wrongs I have done are not hidden from thee.

Psalm 69:5

I know, O LORD, that thy judgments are right,
  and that in faithfulness thou hast afflicted me.

Psalm 119:75

But so quickly the psalmist goes on to magnify the enemies' guilt as greater, and to request their defeat or demise.

Was the psalmist really so innocent? If so, why are there so many psalms of affliction and adversity? If the psalm writers were always so pure, what accounts for the constant trouble they were in? We may well wonder how they made so many enemies in the first place.

Was their world more malevolent than ours? Were they surrounded by more hostile or more devious people than we are today? Or was it perhaps God's fault? Did God fail to protect them adequately when dangers arose? Was God negligent in allowing such enemies to get too close in the first place? Or was it that the Israelites were like children who stumble when the parent lets go, or toddlers who pick up harmful objects when the parent isn't looking?

Was the psalmist really so innocent? It hardly seems likely. To be sure, there were instances when the psalmist could rightly claim not to be at fault. There are times when all of us are falsely accused—and are fiercely aware of it. At just such a time, perhaps, Psalm 17 was composed.

More often, the words of Psalm 143 strike home. Somewhere inside us, we recognize our own impurity. We acknowledge the reality that even if we are innocent in one particular situation, there is enough wrongdoing overall in our lives to have us found guilty.

Primal Goodness

It is as though there were two distinct voices within us. One of them wants to plead innocent even in the face of accusations backed up by hard evidence. Part of this protest stems from fear of punishment. Part of it comes from sheer self-delusion, from our inability or unwillingness to admit wrongdoing.

But another ingredient in this plea is a desire to restate our primal goodness, to affirm our worth and value despite the wrong we have done. We could call this our original-identity complex or our pre-Fall mentality. For somewhere inside us is a memory of what it is to be good, a memory reflected in the intense desire we have to be seen as good by others.

That desire tells us something about the profoundly relational nature of our being. To simply be good is not enough. We also have this fundamental compulsion to be perceived as good in the eyes of others or at least to be accepted by others despite our inability to be wholly good. We need others to affirm something within or about us, which in turn helps us to feel good about ourselves.

Of course, there is a difference between feeling good and actually being good, but in this context they are closely connected. This is our apple-of-the-eye syndrome, our longing for someone somewhere to value us, to confirm our being through the power of love.

Culpability

Then there is the second voice, the voice that speaks to us of our guilt and acknowledges our wrongdoing. This is our post-Fall voice, the voice that begs,

> Enter not into judgment with thy servant;
> for no [one] living is righteous before thee.
>
> Psalm 143:2

It is crucial that we listen to this voice. For to pretend innocence when we know of our guilt is to play a most dangerous game.

Elsewhere, another psalmist writes,

> Behold, the wicked [person] conceives evil,
> and is pregnant with mischief,
> and brings forth lies.
>
> Psalm 7:14

In this pointed portrayal of how evil is born in our lives, are we not all described? For who among us has never been "pregnant with mischief" or given birth to deceit?

This truth about us puts us at risk. For not only does it lead to estrangement from others—indeed, to our becoming enemies ourselves in the eyes of others—it can also lead to more devastating consequences. Put in biblical terms, we risk the wrath of God. Those who do not perceive or acknowledge their failures and faults, their fundamental misorientations in life, may find themselves facing the most fearsome Enemy of all:

> If a man does not repent, God will whet his sword;
>   he has bent and strung his bow;
> he has prepared his deadly weapons,
>   making his arrows fiery shafts.
>
>   Psalm 7:12-13

However we may conceive of God, the cumulative power of that reality, which so exceeds any individual life, can gather against us in ways more destructive than we are capable of imagining. The psalmist when faced with enemies whose power was substantial enough to harm the writer's life, always had God to appeal to in the end. But when that God withdraws, when that God personally decides to oppose us and actually joins forces with our enemies, where then do we go for salvation? We are at that point irrevocably doomed. Thus, the psalmist wisely pleads, even in a psalm that otherwise exudes confidence:

> Turn not thy servant away in anger,
>   thou who hast been my help.
> Cast me not off, forsake me not,
>   O God of my salvation!
>
>   Psalm 27:9

It is better to be engaged in even an imperfect relationship with our Source than to be totally cut off and forsaken. Nothing could be more hopeless than that.

Evil

The last petition of the Lord's Prayer acknowledges this danger that we will give birth to evil in such a way as to finally lead to our own destruction. "Deliver us from evil" refers not only to deliverance from enemies; it also refers to the evil we can do to ourselves.

To pray "Deliver us from evil" is to ask for the strength and wisdom to curb those desires that can destroy both ourselves and others. "Deliver us from evil" is an implicit acknowledgment of our capacity to commit evil in the first place. This, again, is our second voice speaking.

Quite deliberately, that last petition of the Lord's Prayer is followed by a doxology, an expression of praise and thanksgiving. So often, at the end of the psalm writers' laments and petitions come words of promise and praise. It is almost as if praise is an antidote to evil, as if by focusing with a humble spirit on what is good and positive and beyond our own being, we can defend ourselves against the destructive powers within and around us.

> Deliver me from my enemies, O my God, . . .
> deliver me from those who work evil. . . .
> But I will sing of thy might;
> I will sing aloud of thy steadfast love. . . .
> For thou hast been to me a fortress
> and a refuge in the day of my distress.
> O my Strength, I will sing praises to thee.
>
> Psalm 59:1a, 2a, 16, 17a

Caution

Having acknowledged the necessity of heeding this second voice, we need also to note that the accusing voice is sometimes too strong. It can bind us too tightly, overwhelming us with such guilt that even when external absolution is given, it cannot sink in. This, too, is a dangerous state.

To grasp the healing truth, we need to find a balance between the two voices within us. We must acknowledge our failures and our intrinsic imperfection, yet we must not abandon the images of our own goodness.

For the psalm writers and later for the followers of Jesus, this balance was found through the justification that is freely offered by God—not simply forgiveness, but a true and substantial goodness imputed to humanity out of divine love. It was their confidence in divine grace, finally, that gave the psalm writers grounds for hope.

> But thou, O Lord, art a God merciful and gracious,
>   slow to anger and abounding in
>   steadfast love and faithfulness.
>
> Psalm 86:15

> For thy name's sake, O LORD, preserve my life!
>   In thy righteousness bring me out of trouble!
>
> Psalm 143:11

When the divine eyes, the eyes of love, look at us, what they see is not only what we are or have been but what we stand to become. When we can look at each other in a similar fashion, the enemy experiences of our lives will begin to diminish and perhaps one day to disappear. By learning to see ourselves and others with the eyes of love, we may recover some of the innocence for which we so earnestly long.

22

Survival and Recovery

For the enemy has pursued me;
  has crushed my life to the ground;
  . . . [and] has made me to sit in darkness like those long dead.
I remember the days of old,
  I meditate on all that thou hast done;
  I muse on what thy hands have wrought.
Deliver me, O LORD, from my enemies!
  I have fled to thee for refuge!
Teach me to do thy will,
  for thou art my God!
Let thy good spirit lead me
  on a level path!

Psalm 143:3, 5, 9-10

So far, in reflecting upon the reality and power of our enemies, we have thought of them as "other," as persons or forces outside ourselves. But there is another dimension to the "enemy" idea that needs to be considered.

The Enemy Within

Often our enemies are not primarily external. The real enemy may live within. That inner enemy can induce opposition from others as a response to conflicting energies at work inside ourselves.

The enemy within is the most fearsome of all. When the enemy is external—or at least perceived to be—it does not penetrate the inner sanctums of the soul. But to be attacked from within is to have the soul at war with itself.

Often our external enemies are exaggerated. They may even be manufactured by the enemy within—external products of internal conflicts. Projecting these conflicts onto an outside form can make them easier to deal with or even to avoid altogether.

Who is this enemy within? Where does it come from? Sometimes our internal enemy is a reflection of unresolved turmoil remaining from the past—dysfunctional families, low self-esteem, hurts received as a child. Sometimes it is the wounded and angry part of ourselves, still reacting to deep fears instilled in us by abuse or rejection. Or it may be chemical—either the product of chemicals to which we have become addicted or of a natural chemical imbalance.

For each person there can be a different set of explanations for those energies that consume us from within. Some people would include the figure of Satan or demonic influence. Others would include the basic brokenness in us all, as described in the story of the Fall (Gen 3). Most of the time our internal enemies are the combined product of a variety of negative factors.

Wherever the internal enemy comes from, whatever weapons it marshalls against us, its power is undeniable. It can shatter and drain us, sapping our energy and turning us away from constructive activity to self-consuming behaviors. In many ways the enemy within can harm us more than external enemies can.

And sometimes the enemy wins. We are defeated, crushed, ground down. We discover what it means to "sit in darkness like those long dead." In such times of living death when all seems lost and our lives lie shattered in broken pieces around us, it is difficult to discern what, if anything, is left. Yet, at the crushed times, when we have come to the end of our possibilities and sit Job-like on the refuse of our dreams, it is then that we can discover those resources in life that endure.

The Value of Memory

One resource that remains when all else crumbles is memory. It is no accident that at the point when darkness had descended and the enemy had all but obliterated hope, at that very point the psalmist focused on events past:

> I remember the days of old,
> I meditate on all that thou hast done.
>
> Psalm 143:5a

Such remembering serves several functions. One of these is closure. People in their later years often spend substantial time in memories. This can be a process of retreating into happier times, escaping from the less-satisfying realities of the present. It can also be a way of rounding out life's journey.

In a similar way memory serves as a measuring stick by which we evaluate our lives and discern patterns of meaning. By helping us see who we have been, memory can show us who we are now. That knowledge can bring either comfort or shame, or both. But it can also guide us toward change.

Memory serves yet another purpose. By showing us how we have survived or changed in the past, memory can renew our capacity to envision a different future. It reminds us that the present is never final, that there are other realities both behind us and yet to come.

Memory validates our being and proves our existence. It demonstrates that we have lived in the substantial world, interacting with people and forces around us.

In one of its most important functions, memory connects us to tradition. It points us to that collective human experience of which we are a part and from which we derive so much of our identity.

The psalmist, in remembering what God had done, was remembering people, places, and events of generations past. To remember "what thy hands have wrought" was to recall the names and experiences of people like Abraham, David, and Moses—people whose lives signaled deliverance from oppression and doubt. From stories such as these the psalmist could derive courage for believing in deliverance from current trials. Memory formed the sustaining base for endurance and hope. To remember in times of crisis is to engage one of our best and most basic resources for renewal.

Relationships

Another resource often discovered in defeat is our relationships with others. For the psalmist, the critical relationship was with God. Thus, the psalmist's appeal for deliverance was premised on there being a relationship in which God, too, had a stake:

> For thy name's sake, O LORD, preserve my life! . . .
> And in thy steadfast love cut off my enemies, . . .
>   for I am thy servant.
>
> Psalm 143:11a, 12a, c

In times of severe crisis we, like the psalmist, may discover others who have a stake in our recovery, who for the sake of the relationship will invest themselves in our deliverance. To discover such support is both a joy and a relief—it expands our very being. It teaches us the meaning of being fully human. It magnifies the awareness we all need that none of us is totally self-sufficient.

To be delivered through the assistance of a fellow sojourner in life gives birth to a deep kind of gratitude, one which can only come when we have known what the Pit looks like from the inside. Sometimes those who help us have been there themselves, and their experiences have motivated them to help others. At other times, those who take part in our deliverance simply have the willingness and the natural capacity to offer a helping hand.

There is a great strengthening power at work through those who will not abandon us in our time of trial. It is a healing power that penetrates the deepest corners of our darkness and helps to lift us up. The enemy may succeed in pushing us down for a while. But when advocates and friends are present, no enemy can keep us there.

That is the final discovery of the Pit, the other possibility that arises when the crushing is done. Once we have known defeat and survived, our capacity for growth is enlarged.

New Paths

Beyond our failures lie paths upon which we can set our lives once again, given appropriate effort and aid. The psalmist describes it, again in terms of divine assistance:

Teach me to do thy will,
    for thou art my God!
Let thy good spirit lead me
    on a level path!

Psalm 143:10

This image of a level path includes more than the idea of making a fresh start. It also implies a commitment to getting things right next time. It alludes to whole new possibilities for our lives.

To find such a level path and to stay on it requires, as the psalm suggests, continual learning. We need to focus on those instructions and insights that can help us find and stay on the proper path.

Following this level path, as the psalmist tells us, is best achieved by finding a focus outside ourselves, by aligning ourselves with a greater purpose for our lives, and by seeking out those good spirits who can offer positive reinforcement and guidance for our journey.

All in all, the image of a level path beyond the time of crushing is one of the most hopeful that the psalms can offer us. It is a symbol that makes facing enemies considerably less grim, for even when adversaries defeat us, we have not come to our end. The path that leads to the Pit also continues beyond it. On the other side of the abyss, the path levels out and opens up again.

Part III

Words of Assurance

Introduction:
The Faith Behind the Psalms

Praise the LORD!
  Praise the LORD, O my soul!
Put not your trust in [rulers],
  in [mortals], in whom there is no help.
When [their] breath departs [they return] to [the] earth;
  on that very day [their] plans perish.
Happy [are those] . . .
  whose hope is in the LORD [their] God,
who made heaven and earth,
  the sea, and all that is in them;
who keeps faith forever.

Psalm 146:1, 3-4, 5a, 6

All the psalms are written in a very special context. While they put into poetic form some of our deepest human longings and include profoundly stirring reflections on life's wonders and sorrows, they do so within the context of religious faith. They are premised on belief in a loving, powerful Creator who has authored all of life. Behind all the psalms is the conviction of a reality far greater than anything merely human.

That perspective underlies the psalmist's advice to "put not your trust in rulers" or, for that matter, in other mortals. In the psalmist's eyes there is a much more reliable and trustworthy resource for our lives. Naturally, other people may prove to be greatly helpful to us. We certainly all need the resources, support, and companionship that others can give. But no human being—

neither counselor, clergy, spouse, friend, nor politician—can ultimately accomplish our full deliverance for us.

Implicit in this perspective is not only faith in a divine being but a corresponding awareness of human finitude—an understanding of human limitation, human vulnerability, and human fallibility. At the same time, there is a profound awareness of the transience and unpredictability of life.

> When [our] breath departs, [we return] to [the] earth;
> on that very day [our] plans perish.
>
> Psalm 146:4

By definition, to be human is to be finite. Our existence is always only temporary. We are limited creatures.

> As for [mortals, our] days are like grass;
> [we flourish] like a flower of the field;
> for the wind passes over it, and it is gone,
> and its place knows it no more.
>
> Psalm 103:15-16

> [Those] of low estate are but a breath,
> [those] of high estate are a delusion;
> in the balances they go up;
> they are together lighter than a breath.
>
> Psalm 62:9

In God the psalmists saw permanence. In God they found meaning and hope. But these were not merely random projections or creative compensations for their own inadequacies. The psalmists belonged to a tradition that claimed to have directly experienced God. This experience revealed not just an abstract, benevolent deity who provided order and direction for life and justification for social conventions. Their experience of God took them into an understanding of God as very personal, very caring, and passionately involved in their life and history.

God for the Hebrews was more than a cosmic benefactor or divine defender in times of war, although God was that, too. That the psalmist's God went beyond such basic functions of divinity is evident in the view that God actually has a personal commitment to humankind. In the qualities of love, compassion, jealousy, and even anger, God moves beyond the merely functional to the intensely relational. That is why all the cries of the psalmist make sense. They were made with the assumption that there was a God who could and would take them seriously.

This attitude shows through in passages that reflect some of the earliest memories of Israel's existence as a people: "And the people of Israel groaned under their bondage, and cried out for help, and their cry under bondage came up to God. And God heard their groaning, and God remembered [the] covenant with Abraham, with Isaac, and with Jacob. And God saw the people of Israel, and God knew their condition" (Exod 2:23b-25). The verbs in this passage are striking. They describe an active, responsive God to whom human sorrows are important. This is the kind of God the psalm writers addressed.

Indeed, they developed this imagery even more specifically:

> Happy is [the one] whose help is the God . . .
>   who keeps faith for ever;
>   who executes justice for the oppressed;
>   who gives food to the hungry.
> The LORD sets the prisoners free;
>   the LORD opens the eyes of the blind.
> The LORD lifts up those who are bowed down;
>   the LORD loves the righteous.
> The LORD watches over the sojourners,
>   [and] upholds the widow and the fatherless.
>
> Psalm 146:5a, 6b, 7-9b

> [God] heals the brokenhearted,
>   and binds up their wounds. . . .
> The LORD lifts up the downtrodden,
>   [and] casts the wicked to the ground.
>
> Psalm 147:3, 6

> The LORD upholds all who are falling,
>   and raises up all who are bowed down.

The eyes of all look to thee,
and thou givest them their food in due season. . . .
[God] fulfills the desire of all who fear him,
[God] also hears their cry, and saves them.

Psalm 145:14-15, 19

These passages show us what the psalmists had come to expect from God and, indeed, who they understood God to be. This is a God before whom we may place our most personal cries. This is a God who cares. What's more, this is a God who takes a special interest in those who are downtrodden, weak, or abandoned, those who are weighed down by the burdens and inequities of life. For believers now, as when the psalms were written, that is a particularly good kind of news.

Human experience demonstrates, however, that the God-believer relationship is neither automatic nor predictable. In their deep faith the psalmists gave God credit for providence and protection. Yet in their day-to-day reality (as in ours), they often experienced difficulty, conflict, and deprivation. According to the biblical record itself, God may be the ultimate resource for all the gifts of life, yet God clearly does not function as a divine magician who dispenses favors on command. There is a persistent tension between the faith that sees God as provider and the experiences of life that testify to unfulfilled needs. That tension is never fully resolved either in Scripture or in the religions that grow out of it. We are left standing in a mystery.

Change

Despite that fact, the Old Testament writers remained confident in God's existence and in God's power to effect change, both in the life of the believer and in human history in general.

Great is our LORD, and abundant in power;
[God's] understanding is beyond measure.

Psalm 147:5

It is one of the strengths of such faith that it offers alternatives, that it provides visions of change. Instead of being stuck in fatalism or nihilism, the psalmists hold up the idea that life can be different—and not only different but better. Suffering and oppression are not immutable conditions. The psalmists' vision of God provides a way to believe that change is possible. In itself, this is a profound, highly motivating concept.

Yet the Old Testament writers went a step further. They describe God as One who not only can cause change but who can also redeem negative situations. God has the power to bring good out of evil, gain out of loss. This idea is evident in the great story of Israel's deliverance from slavery in Egypt and in the individual lives of such people as Joseph, who told the brothers who betrayed him, "As for you, you meant evil against me; but God meant it for good" (Gen 50:20a).

The idea that both change and redemption are possible can help lift us out of despair. It helps us see that no situation is a complete dead end, devoid of redeeming possibilities. Such a vision produces hope and gives us courage to act despite our fears.

In these ways the psalm writers' vision of God serves a constructive purpose. But these writers were interested in more than manufacturing a useful popular psychology or some kind of practical motivational therapy. They were committed to the being and the meaning of a personal God. What their psalms portray for us is a strong personal relationship, an intimacy with the divine being that gave comfort, courage, and a sense of purpose. These psalms were all written from the perspective that in God hope was not only possible but boundless.

Expectations

At times this faith expressed itself in anguish and anger at God for not acting as expected, for not acting more swiftly, or for not acting at all. The psalmists even dared to nudge and cajole God into action with the suggestion that God was asleep on the job!

> Arise, O LORD, in thy anger,
>   lift thyself up against the fury of my enemies;
>   awake, O my God; . . .
>
> Psalm 7:6a

What we sense in such sentiments is not only a particular faith structure at work but a marvelous sense of intimate relationship between the human and the All-Powerful. The nature and quality of this relationship is obvious in the very fact that it allowed the psalmists to bring into their discussions with God every aspect of daily life, from practical needs and national political interests to their deepest personal sorrows and their anger, bitterness, and jealousy, not to mention such positive experiences as thanksgiving and the sheer joy of living, all of which overflowed into worship. Given such dynamism, it is no wonder that this faith has shown such vitality and lasted so long.

For us as for the psalm writers, God remains the ultimate sanctuary when all other options in life are exhausted. God is the one place in all the universe where we humans can go to find a door open and love waiting with a promise of redemption.

Yet, this was no stop-gap theology whereby God was a useful last resort to be saved until desperately needed. To the contrary, the psalm writers understood God to be one who by nature is involved in daily life for guidance and healing.

Cost

The Old Testament writers also understood that God's involvement is not cheap. Indeed, it is very costly. For to be so involved in the mess of human existence—the failure, the fickleness, the violence, the betrayals, the corruption, and the destruction—all this pains even God, who is known as the author of justice and righteousness and as One who profoundly loves humanity, who suffers deeply with us as we suffer. Indeed, the prophets of the Old Testament portray God as alternately livid with anger over the corruptions of human existence and torn with anguish over those loved ones who have so badly failed:

> How can I give you up . . . !
> My heart recoils within me,
>   my compassion grows warm and tender.
> I will not execute my fierce anger.
>
> Hosea 11:8a, c, 9a

In the New Testament, the nature and extent of God's extraordinary love culminates in God's own child being sacrificed in a most dramatic and excruciating death for the redemption of humankind.

This whole concept of such an extensive, love-based relationship between humanity and the divine is virtually unique in the annals of human religion. So powerful has it proved that today nearly a quarter of humanity claims affiliation with this faith. This same relationship of love was the motivating premise of the psalm writers, providing the basis for these words to which we turn yet today.

Context

Not everyone shares the psalmists' faith. We cannot all claim to be products of their tradition. Yet to have an informed understanding of the context in which the psalms were formed and their intended meaning, we need to be aware of this background. Even those who do not share the psalmists' faith can find a measure of wisdom and comfort in their words.

In the meditations on assurance and hope, traditional biblical faith comes to the fore. In these Scripture passages we will see how the psalmists' faith was played out in positive images. Hopefully, these images will prove valuable even for those who are not as close to this unique faith tradition.

We have seen how the words of affliction and adversity that the psalms provide can console and strengthen us. From here on we may discover words of assurance and affirmation that can also assist us in climbing out of our pits, words that can help us learn how to celebrate life again. To live in full health requires that beyond the words of affliction we also lay claim to the words of hope that are there for us. These, too, are words we need to speak, both for our own well being and for that of others.

23

Delusion and Deliverance

If it had not been the LORD who was on our side,
  when [enemies] rose up against us,
then they would have swallowed us up alive,
  when their anger was kindled against us;
then the flood would have swept us away, . . .
then over us would have gone
  the raging waters.
Blessed be the LORD,
  who has not given us
  as prey to their teeth!
We have escaped as a bird
  from the snare of the fowlers;
the snare is broken,
  and we have escaped!
Our help is in the name of the LORD,
  who made heaven and earth.

Psalm 124:2-4a, 5, 6-8

God Against Us

One of the greatest delusions in the world is that God is on our side. Innumerable atrocities have been committed on the basis of this delusion. All kinds of social, ecclesiological, and interpersonal abuses have been carried out with the justification that God approved or would at least look the other way. Actions that would otherwise be considered manipulative, immoral, or destructive have often been sanctified by declaring that they are done in the name of God.

The Christian Church is no doubt the greatest arena of such abuse. In the name of God, the Church and its leaders have burned people at the stake, supported military and cultural imperialism around the globe, and forced countless people to submit to arbitrary policies and practices at odds with the very gospel the Church exists to proclaim.

At the same time it must be said that the Church has been one of the greatest arenas of grace in human history, acting as a force for liberation, social justice, and personal comfort for untold millions of people. The Church has been the seedbed in which many of humanity's greatest aspirations have flowered—in art, literature, music—and in which countless lives have been poured out for the good of others.

But the flip side of the Church, its grim failures and sins, demonstrate the danger of an unqualified belief that God is inevitably on any given side. Ultimately, *God* is the one who chooses which side to be on, and according to biblical paradigms, God's choice is most often the one where justice, peace, and grace are served. This means that God may choose sides against us as well as for us. God may even work outside the community of faith with and through people who do not subscribe to the biblical faith or acknowledge God at all. That possibility is well established in Scripture; for example, the pagan king Cyrus being designated as God's anointed servant (Isa 45:1), or Jesus' numerous references to and affirmations of non-Israelites as recipients of God's grace, or even the inclusion of Gentiles in the early Christian Church.

It is in God's own nature to be free to choose whatever sides serve God's purposes. That choosing, however, has been qualified by commitments that God has previously made. According to Scripture, God has already made commitments to the people of Israel, who in the New Testament are understood to include those who follow Jesus.

But those divine commitments do not obligate God to serve as anyone's lackey or the rubber stamp of the believing community's decisions. God is no supernatural genie to be stroked out of an ecclesiastical bottle and commanded to fulfill the wishes of self-oriented individuals or groups. We are God's servants; not God, ours.

The mentality that sees God as a heavenly delivery service at our disposal is the mentality that produces the delusion that God is automatically on our side. It is a demonic mentality capable of causing great harm to ourselves and to others.

God for Us

These negative possibilities exist because the positive one does, namely, that God can indeed be on our side. Such was the psalm writer's experience. Here was a case where without God, or so the psalmist was convinced, all would have been lost. Had God not been on their side, the psalmist's community would have been defeated and dissolved. They were utterly vulnerable, fragile, and without recourse. It was precisely in that awareness that they came to experience deliverance.

Their experience shows us the potential of God's favor. For when God actually *is* on our side, that can be life's greatest hope. Perhaps the clue to whether God is with us or not lies in our expectations. If we are awaiting a God who will always serve our immediate interests, then we are likely to be disappointed. If, however, the God in whom we trust is the one defined by Scripture as the God of justice and love, then we may reasonably expect God's presence, assuming that our agenda is one of grace and justice and trust in the ultimately salvific purpose of this loving God.

Paradox

In such a scenario we seem forced to give up our independence, to abandon completely free choice. We appear reduced to a vulnerability that could even expose us to further suffering.

Yet that is exactly the kind of faith modeled in Scripture as most to our advantage in the long run. It is the explicit paradox of Scripture that when we are most vulnerable, God is most powerful. The life willingly lost is the one most profoundly saved. God's strength is perfected in weakness.

Incredible as that may seem to human logic, it is the testimony of Scripture that in such a way divine salvation occurs. This is the astounding secret of biblical faith.

None of this is to say that God is not powerful in human terms. Scripture and tradition demonstrate that, indeed, God's power is quite real and historical. But the power here represented is very different from what we commonly expect.

Release

The psalmists experienced God's power firsthand. On the edge of destruction they discovered deliverance. At the point where hope seemed lost and doom inevitable, they were whisked away from danger and freed from whatever threatened to destroy them.

The images used to describe this experience are almost giddy. They depict relief, delight, a soaring sense of freedom like that of a bird released from a cage or a captured animal let out of a trap.

> Blessed be the LORD,
>   who has not given us
>   as prey to their teeth!
> We have escaped as a bird
>   from the snare of the fowlers;
> the snare is broken,
>   and we have escaped!
>
> Psalm 124:6-7

After all the experiences of gloom and sorrow depicted in some of the psalms we have surveyed, it is a breath of fresh air to read these words of release. They represent not just the possibility of deliverance but its actuality. Here is an account of prayer answered, of deliverance that actually occurred.

The escape imagery is particularly appropriate, for escape is what we long for in times of pressure, when we feel hemmed in and afflicted. As another psalmist expressed it:

> And I say, "O that I had wings like a dove!
>   I would fly away and be at rest; . . .

> I would haste to find me a shelter
> from the raging wind and tempest."
>
> Psalm 55:6, 8

Escape is an image we need. It is a way of imagining not only deliverance but transition from a captive past to a clean, new future.

It is good to read in Psalm 124 of a case where escape was accomplished. It is good to hear of someone making it, being delivered from difficult circumstances. That knowledge gives us hope for our own situation.

The psalmist concludes with a statement of faith, giving credit to the source of deliverance, the One who made the breakaway possible.

> Our help is in the name of the LORD,
> who made heaven and earth.
>
> Psalm 124:8

In this proclamation the psalmist does more than merely give thanks. There is also the deeper message about this Lord who arranges escapes, the message that this Lord is the Lord of help, not of suffering. It is in the very character of God and in the nature of the relationship between God and God's people that God desires to be a source of healing and assistance, not destruction. This maker of heaven and earth is first of all a creator, not a destroyer. This God is One who eagerly and gladly desires to be on our side in the end.

24

Guidance and Protection

The LORD is my shepherd, I shall not want;
he makes me lie down in green pastures.
He leads me beside still waters;
he restores my soul.
He leads me in paths of righteousness
for his name's sake.
Even though I walk through the valley of the shadow of death,
I fear no evil;
for thou art with me;
thy rod and thy staff,
they comfort me.
Thou preparest a table before me
in the presence of my enemies;
thou anointest my head with oil,
my cup overflows.
Surely goodness and mercy shall follow me
all the days of my life;
and I shall dwell in the house of the LORD
for ever.

Psalm 23

Why is this psalm so popular? Why do people love it so much? Perhaps it is because it pushes such basic buttons inside each of us. All of us experience fear and death; all of us have wants; all of us at some time or another face alienation, isolation, or insecurity. And at some point in our life, each of us walks through valleys of deep darkness.

As a result, we all long for company and comfort. We do not want to be alone. We like the idea that Someone is watching over us, in the way a parent might sit at the bedside of a child.

This psalm taps our longing for protection. It gently conjures up a sense of innocence and vulnerability surrounded by an affirmation of providence and security. It offers a vision of peace in contrast to all the warring experiences of our lives. It is a psalm of respite, a brilliant collection of images which together provide a place for the heart to go for laying aside life's worries, for simply soaking in a sphere of serenity.

This psalm also speaks of overcoming fear. So much of our lives is dominated by fear. We fear failure; we fear loneliness and rejection; we fear our own powerlessness. We fear the countless threats that living brings. We know full well how vulnerable we are to the violence, inequities, tragedies, and accidents of human existence. In response, this psalm gives us an image of fears overcome, of threats removed and kept at a distance.

Who does not long to lie down where the waters are still, where life, at least for a while, is no longer disturbed by the eddies and currents of everyday life? True, rushing waters can be energizing, and we love to ride the waves and even to be lifted to the crest. But when the waves come crashing down upon us or great wakes threaten to capsize us, then it is the still waters we seek. The image of a soothing rest by a peaceful pool is hard to resist.

Similarly, the image of green pastures is an image of calm. But it is much more. It is an image of well-being. Green pastures are comfortable places where we are well provided for, places where our needs are met.

That there is one who would lead us to such places, that there is one who desires and intends such satisfaction for us in life, is an appealing thought. Not to want but to be provided for by one who means us well is a lovely idea. Perhaps, it taps our desire for security or calls to mind the comfort we associate with whomever it is that has been a provider in our life or, at least, with our longing for such a provider.

But it is not only the sense of having needs satisfied that appeals. It is also the sense that someone cares for us so much as to want that for us and to provide it.

Courage and Company

One of the great strengths of this psalm is the comfort and courage it gives for facing times of darkness. The valley of the shadow of death is a place most of us know too well. Death's shadow casts itself over our lives when loved ones or we ourselves come to life's end. Death's shadow is also present when relationships are injured, jobs and homes broken, dreams lost. It is the nature of life that death can infiltrate every aspect of life, casting its shadow at will.

But the psalmist lifts up for us the vision of One who will walk with us through the valleys. Psalm 23 offers us the assurance that we need not be alone in the shadow times. In fact, this whole psalm is an image of comfort—of help in difficult times, of peace even in the midst of life's turmoil.

Even the table prepared in the presence of enemies is a symbol of peace. Surprisingly, perhaps, the psalm does not promise that enemies will disappear. Instead, it assumes their continued presence in our lives. But what the psalm does describe is an inner tranquility no matter what external forces may be arrayed against us. In a sense, this is a Zen kind of psalm: It offers an image of transcendence as well as of deliverance.

The premise of the whole psalm, of course, is contained in the image of shepherd and flock. By definition, the shepherd is protector, guide, and companion for the journey. The shepherd leads the protected ones to places of nourishment, refreshment, and peace and fends off whatever threatens the flock's well-being. For those who are afraid, hurting, lonely, or simply seeking to find words for their experiences of confidence and tranquility, this is a marvelously comforting, expressive psalm.

Dependency

But it raises a question. In these days of relational analysis when all our attitudes and relationships are constantly called into question by whatever psychological theory is in vogue, can we trust what this psalm expresses? Or does this treasure of human faith and longing describe a sick dependency? Instead of a shepherd, should we be turning to a therapist who can lead us away from such fantasies?

The meaning of "dependency" varies with the person using the term. Usually it implies something unhealthy, for example, attachment to drugs, alcohol, a certain kind of activity, or even to another person or group. To be sure, unhealthy dependencies are not only possible in life; they are pervasive. We all have some. Insofar as "dependency" is a useful term in liberating people from unhealthy relationships, it is certainly a constructive one.

But what about the psalmist? Was this person overly dependent on God? To describe God as a shepherd and to attribute to the shepherd such caretaking behavior—is that not a step in the direction of dependency? Would we not be better off to distance ourselves from such a caregiver and to take care of ourselves instead? Can't we find our own still waters and create our own green pastures? Isn't fear something we need to conquer by ourselves, without recourse to a protector God? Doesn't the ultimate expression of our independence and inner tranquility come from daring to set our own table in the presence of enemies and to fashion our own private goodness and mercy? Wouldn't that be the modern, American ideal?

No doubt, many would say yes. Many would disdain this shepherd imagery as an immature kind of religious dependency. It is a manifestation of modern Western culture—a culture that has reduced human identity from clan to community to nuclear family and, most recently, to single units—that the model of health and success is unqualified, utter, personal independence.

But others would argue that being fully human requires being fully in relationship, which includes an inevitable degree of dependency. For at its best, dependency is an openness that engenders growth, just as, at its worst, it is an imprisonment that stultifies development.

To be dependent in healthy ways is good. None of us, after all, is ever totally independent. We are all products of relationships and always will be defined by those people and events around us with whom we have no choice but to interact.

If the term "dependency" refers to unhealthy attachments and its use helps to free us from them, then it is a good conceptual tool. If "freedom from dependency" means utter disconnectedness from others, including the interdependency necessary to human growth and identity, it undermines both physical and spiritual health. Not to be interactive, not to be engaged in vulnerable ways with other humans is to be headed toward nonbeing.

It is a fallacy to imagine that we can engage in relationships with a kind of calculated distance, exercising purely autonomous control. Granted, we need to reflect more fully on our relationships: their nature, content, and direction; what we bring to and receive from them; and what is healthy or unhealthy about them. But to imagine that we can ever have perfectly understood and directed relationships is a delusion. Such a desire masks a deep insecurity and a failure to understand the gifts and opportunities of engaging in relationship.

Celebration

So how about our shepherd relationships? Can we sing this psalm and celebrate the vision it offers us? Of course we can! Its gift to us is a wonderful picture of peace, comfort, and a healthy, healing relationship. No matter how we might analyze, criticize, or psychologize it, its magic will remain. For centuries past and for as long as people continue to read it, this psalm will embrace those who let it with its beautiful pastoral imagery, transporting them to places of hope and peace. Its sense of intimacy, its ability to make us feel loved, valued, and protected without any preconditions or demands will continue to speak comfort to the human soul.

Does it also guarantee happiness? Does it promise goodness and mercy as automatic gifts? No. In fact, it is interesting to note that goodness and mercy are designated as benefits that *follow* from the choices made and the trust given in the psalm as a whole. They are part of the commitment the psalmist makes "to dwell in the house of the Lord forever."

For us as for the psalmist, goodness and mercy are not random gifts but specific results of the choices we make and the trusts we offer in life. They come as a consequence of how we live out the visions that guide us. But that they can indeed be ours is what the psalm so confidently conveys.

All in all, this psalm stands as a timelessly beautiful testimony to the comfort beyond affliction, the deliverance out of oppression, the affirmation of our dreams for a life of security and blessing. It is a healing retreat for the wounded soul. As we enter or as we emerge from our valleys of darkness, these are good words to know.

25

Restored

When the LORD restored the fortunes of Zion,
  we were like those who dream.
Then our mouth was filled with laughter,
  and our tongue with shouts of joy. . . .
The LORD has done great things for us;
  we are glad.
Restore our fortunes, O LORD, . . .
May those who sow in tears
  reap with shouts of joy!
[Those who go] forth weeping,
  bearing the seed for sowing,
shall come home with shouts of joy,
  bringing [their] sheaves with [them].

Psalm 126:1-2a, 3, 4a, 5-6

How badly we need dreams! Dreams carry us to places of comfort and hope. They release us from the confines of whatever realities oppress us or threaten to crush us. In dreams we find motivation for enduring, inspiration for persevering against the obstacles that confront us. Dreams are a way we envision the future and motivate ourselves to achieve it. At the very least, they help us survive until the future arrives. Without dreams the human spirit would shrivel and die.

Only rarely do dreams live up to our expectations. When our dreams do come true, it is usually with less excitement than we have anticipated. Often, because dreams reach fruition gradually,

135

because they are partially the product of our own patient effort over extended periods of time, they may arrive quietly, almost unnoticed. Sometimes we don't even realize that our dreams have come true until we pause and look back, remembering where we have been and recalling what our dreams were in the first place. We may even be a trifle disappointed.

But not so in the psalmist's case! This was one occasion when the dream exceeded expectations. What the psalmist's community experienced was so powerful, so fulfilling, so exceedingly positive and welcome, they could hardly believe it, and they responded with unrestrained joy and outright laughter. It was too good to be true!

It was also one of those experiences for which most of us long with all our hearts, especially when we have been to the bottom, when we have seen our dearest dreams lying shattered at our feet. Only the mouth that has drunk the bitter dregs of failure and loss can fully appreciate that sweet taste of freedom and deliverance. Only the scarred and broken heart can pump the new blood of a healed and restored life.

Being restored after being downtrodden generates a power no words can convey. The uplifting energy of being liberated from a long and dismal captivity moves the soul as does little else in this life. It reveals a special depth in the human capacity for emotion.

Behind the experience described in the psalm was clearly an experience of suffering and loss. Life had been shattered; dreams had been broken; community had been disrupted. In so many instances in our human history, the period of brokenness has been long and profound. Many generations may pass between the initial experience of shattering and the fulfillment of the dream. The Israelites in Egypt and later in Babylon, the African slaves in the Americas, people today in places like Central America and South Africa—all these are examples of people whose suffering continues for generations while they wait for dreams to be fulfilled.

Those who have inherited special dreams and kept them alive know a deeper joy because of their heritage when those dreams are finally fulfilled. But as custodians of such dreams they also carry a deeper sorrow, a lingering melancholy born of the memory of those who suffered without tasting the fruits of deliverance.

A dream of this sort is a community affair. When the harvest comes and the sheaves of rejoicing are brought home, both the celebration and the mourning that must be part of it will be deeper. They who celebrate do so not only for themselves but for all who lived in expectation of the dream coming true.

There is a kind of communal mourning and celebration for individuals, too, even when the losses and recoveries are private. For we read the prayer that those who sow in tears may reap with joy, and we know that it applies to others besides ourselves. There is no monopoly on tears. Life brings us all too many.

Seeds

There is another image of great depth and power in the psalm, one that can carry us from tears of sorrow to tears of joy. This is the image of transformation found in the psalm's affirmation:

> [Those who go] forth weeping,
>   bearing the seed for sowing,
> shall come home with shouts of joy,
>   bringing [their] sheaves with [them].
>
> Psalm 126:6

The very seeds that signaled the bearer's burden become the instruments of deliverance. There is in suffering itself the seed of our restoration.

It is one of the profound mysteries of life that suffering can produce good, that out of pain can come healing. It takes exceptional faith and vision to see in our suffering a seed planted for the sake of our future. That such a seed, watered with our own weeping, can become a source of strength and nourishment seems beyond imagining. Yet, that is exactly the testimony of countless people before us.

That is not to say that suffering is good. But it is to say that the life that flows through our souls is capable of transforming even that which afflicts us into something positive. For when there is a vision, when dreams remain, when we do not lose our capacity to forgive and to fully engage with one another, then our suffering can indeed become a seed that produces good fruit.

Beyond the ache and sweat of cultivating suffering's dark soil there is the dream that our suffering will produce a worthwhile harvest. The same black earth that buries our dreams is a womb that gives them new life. The ground that must be broken by our toil is the foundation in which our future takes root.

Transformation

In order to grow and produce fruit, our seeds must first be cast into the gloomy loam, covered over in darkness and allowed to burst. New life requires this transformation—what emerges will be different from what was sown. But it will be the food of new dreams, a harvest of hope for a new kind of life.

To see in our suffering the seeds of new dreams can help us to endure the suffering. But that requires trusting the power of transformation that flows through all life. It is a matter of combining our internal resources for changing old attitudes and behaviors with an openness to the greater flow of life around us. The psalmist understood that life-power to be God and was not ashamed to attribute to God the power of deliverance.

Our final restoration must come from outside, at least in part. For, when we are pressed to the limits, when all our resources are channeled into mere survival, we must depend on resources beyond ourselves to help achieve that for which we dream. To be open to such external assistance is hardly a reason for shame. It may well be the beginning of true self-realization.

Our restoration needs to have a public dimension, especially when our humiliation and grief have been public. In that way our own deliverance becomes a witness for others.

> Then they said among the nations,
>   "The LORD has done great things for them."
>
> Psalm 126:2b

Indeed, when the dream is fulfilled it becomes a community event, as our own joy flows into the connections we have with others.

It is appropriate that we share this joy with others, for it is part of our human responsibility that we witness to this grace we have received.

These words of the psalmist become a benediction that we can pronounce for all those who suffer. We, too, can speak to others in a vision of transformation:

> May those who sow in tears
> reap with shouts of joy!
>
> Psalm 126:5

26

Exposed

O LORD, thou hast searched me and known me!
Thou knowest when I sit down and when I rise up;
  thou discernest my thoughts from afar.
Thou searchest out my path and my lying down,
  and art acquainted with all my ways.
Even before a word is on my tongue,
  lo, O LORD, thou knowest it altogether. . . .
Whither shall I go from thy Spirit?
  Or whither shall I flee from thy presence?
If I ascend to heaven, thou art there!
  If I make my bed in Sheol, thou art there!
If I take the wings of the morning
  and dwell in the uttermost parts of the sea,
even there thy hand shall lead me,
  and thy right hand shall hold me.
If I say, "Let only darkness cover me,
  and the light about me be night,"
even the darkness is not dark to thee,
  the night is bright as the day;
  for darkness is as light with thee.

Psalm 139:1-4, 7-12

One of things we fear most is being exposed. There are always parts
of us that we would prefer others not see. There are parts of us
we would rather not see ourselves.

Why are we so afraid? What is it that scares us about looking into the deeper reaches of our being? Understandably, there are certain actions or behaviors that we are reluctant to expose to public view. The mistakes and failures of the past or personal habits that might embarrass us are the sort of thing we would not like to uncover. We are not likely to relish revealing to others those aspects of ourselves with which we are not comfortable.

One reason for our self-protective posture is our fear of rejection. For deeper even than our fear of exposure is our need for acceptance. We want to be known and loved.

Therein lies the paradox. On the one hand, we long to be fully known and loved. On the other hand, we fear that exposure will condemn us. It is a dilemma that affects not only our relationships with other people but also our acceptance of ourselves.

Often in times of stress or affliction, we wistfully plead, "If only people knew the real me. . . ." Behind that longing is actually a statement of self-affirmation, a belief that there are good things about us to be known. At the same time, there are pieces of ourselves we would rather hide, secrets so deep we hardly dare acknowledge them even to ourselves.

There are parts of ourselves we do not love and are afraid to accept. They may have to do with actions, behaviors, or attitudes that cause us shame. They may be the products of self-hate, or they may be judgmental messages that we have been carrying for years. Whatever their origin, their effect is to hold us captive in ways that limit both our interactions with others and our acceptance of ourselves.

Sometimes we come to a point where we must face the hidden sides of our psyche. They have cost us too much. We are simply tired of carrying their invisible burdens. When that happens, we often discover not only that the load can be shed but that we are not destroyed by dumping it. The process of clearing out the garbage may be painful, but it can also be healing. We may even be able to make friends with those sides of ourselves that have previously been at war with us. Indeed, to do so can make us stronger by giving us a greater sense of balance or completeness.

In truth, we do want to know ourselves. At the very least, we want to know enough about ourselves to increase our sense of control over our lives and to protect ourselves from whatever it is we fear in our relations with others.

Also, we are curious. There is a part of us that has an almost clinical curiosity about what makes us tick and how that affects who we are. That explains why self-analysis articles are so abundant in popular magazines. It is no coincidence that the stores where we shop for the food we need to survive also sell information about ourselves and our relationships. Both kinds of daily bread are integral to wholeness.

We really do want to know who we are and why. Sometimes that is a deep spiritual quest that plays itself out in religious or philosophical searching. Sometimes we look for answers in horoscopes, palm readings, or other such ancient pursuits. Part of us is afraid of what we will find. Part of us hungers for the truth of our own being, even when that becomes uncomfortable.

Socially, because we are afraid that our dark sides, our weaknesses, or our faults may prevent others from accepting us, we cover them over or deny them. In day-to-day life that is often a practical necessity, for our faults often do alienate others. But those who know us well usually discern our imperfections and choose to accept us anyway. Indeed, it is surprising that being accepted by others despite our faults does not give us more courage to accept ourselves. Yet for many that is a discovery that takes time to absorb.

The truth is that at some deep level we do all long to be free—free from the secrets, free from the judgments, free from the fears that limit our lives. It takes so much energy to hold all the secrets and fears inside. For that reason being exposed can come as a welcome relief. Seen in that light, being exposed is not only one of our greatest fears but also one of our greatest hopes. It can bring us both knowledge and peace.

Healing Exposure

It is in that sense that this psalm recounts being exposed to God. There is an intimacy here that, in the end, proves to be healing and a being known for which the psalmist gives thanks.

At first we might get a different impression. To read, "O Lord, thou hast searched me and known me" could make us nervous. Is that good news or bad? Will we suffer for what has been revealed, or will we be affirmed?

> Thou knowest when I sit down and when I rise up;
>   thou discernest my thoughts. . . .
> Even before a word is on my tongue, . . .
>   lo, O Lord, thou knowest it altogether.
>
> Psalm 139:2, 4

Is not this picture of God a little scary? After all, what is left of privacy when we are so exposed? Does this mean that we have no independent control over our words, thoughts, and feelings? That they are somehow predestined? And what about the psalmist's efforts to flee God's all-penetrating vision?

> Whither shall I go from thy Spirit?
>   Or whither shall I flee from thy presence? . . .
> If I say, "Let only darkness cover me, . . ."
>   even the darkness is not dark to thee.
>
> Psalm 139:7a, 11a, 12a

If God can so easily see into every corner of our lives, where can we hide our shame? How can we have integrity when our independence seems so curtailed? Does independence consist of being able to hide in the first place?

It was not the psalmist's intention to depict a game of cosmic hide-and-seek. This is no picture of an oppressive, nosy God chasing us down for punishment and humiliation. The God of Scripture is hardly so petty or mean.

The psalmist's point is not that we lose our privacy, independence, or self-respect when we are known so fully. Rather, it is that in such knowing we discover our full identity. We cannot flee from the truth. We cannot hide from who we are. Whether we conceive of truth as our reflection in the eyes of the divine or as the image mirrored in the recesses of our own subconscious, it is our whole self with which we must deal and from whom no escape is possible.

For the psalmist, to be fully exposed to God is ultimately positive; that we can never pass beyond the boundaries of God's consciousness is tremendously good news. For it means, according to Scripture's definition of God, that we can never go beyond the realm of love. Wherever we flee, wherever life takes us, in shipwrecks and successes alike, the power of love and redemption will always be there.

In the psalmist's experience of exposure, there are benefits in being so fully known. That there is One who knows us, that there are others who share our pain and understand our needs, who witness our trials and triumphs, means that we are not alone. To be known is to be accompanied. It is to have an understanding and supportive presence for the journey.

To be so known is also to have resources upon which to draw. Those who know us can give us feedback, support, and guidance. But they can also give us something that may never fully come in any other way. For it is those who know us most intimately, who know our worst qualities and greatest mistakes who can mediate the fullest forgiveness to us. Of course, we can forgive ourselves and certainly need to, in order to recover from our setbacks and failings. But that word of absolution that comes from outside, spoken by a trusted ally or authority, can reach us in ways that self-affirmation cannot. The pronouncement of forgiveness gives concrete form to the healing we have needed and found. Only by being known can it be made complete.

Free

In the end, what the psalmist experienced was that to be so fully exposed, so intimately known, was both comforting and liberating. Exposure brought cleansing, a more profound self-awareness, and a greater wonder both at our interconnectedness with others and at life itself.

Like the psalmist, we too may find that the process of becoming more fully exposed and more intimately known is a healthy, uplifting experience. Sometimes when we are the most exposed, we are the most free. We are the most open to healing and to healthy relating, and when we find acceptance and affirmation, we are the most secure.

It is as Jesus once said in another context, "You will know the truth and the truth will make you free" (John 8:32).

27

Confession

To thee, O LORD, I lift up my soul.
O, my God, in thee I trust,
  let me not be put to shame;
  let not my enemies exult over me.
Yea, let none that wait for thee be put to shame;
  let them be ashamed who are wantonly treacherous.
Make me to know thy ways, O LORD;
  teach me thy paths.
Lead me in thy truth and teach me. . . .
Remember not the sins of my youth, or my transgressions;
  according to thy steadfast love remember me,
  for thy goodness' sake, O LORD! . . .
For thy name's sake, O LORD,
  pardon my guilt, for it is great. . . .
Relieve the troubles of my heart,
  and bring me out of my distresses.
Consider my affliction and my trouble,
  and forgive all my sins.
Consider how many are my foes,
  and with what violent hatred they hate me. . . .
Redeem Israel, O God,
  out of all [trouble].

Psalm 25:1-5a, 7, 11, 17-19, 22

Passion is common in the psalms. Some of them roar with anger. Others overflow with gratitude and praise. Some are sublime, others blunt. A few throb with the raw anguish and pathos of the human spirit. Psalm 25 is one of these.

In this complex psalm we encounter both a constant theme and conflicting emotions. We find anger, grief, guilt, hope, and a deep yearning that God will graciously respond. Behind this psalm, clearly, is a painful struggle in which the psalmist must face personal failure, harsh opposition, and the whole question of God's capacity and willingness to give aid in times of trial.

Our Soul

As a first step toward enlisting God's aid, the psalmist cries, "To thee, O Lord, I lift up my soul." Our soul is what we lift up when nothing else is left, when we have been stripped to the core of our being. Our soul is our essence. It is all we have, finally, with which to appeal to Divine Providence.

When we expose and lift up our soul, it usually means that we have exhausted our alternatives. We have tried all the bribes and bargaining ploys we could conceive. Only when false pride is shredded and our external resources used up, when illusions and delusions alike have crumbled, only then do we face our nakedness before the cosmos and seek that awesome, promise-full power that is utterly beyond us. At such a time we stand like cracked crystal before the Artisan of the universe, waiting to be glued back together or melted down and recast completely.

To stand so exposed is as close as we come to purity. When the fire in our soul combines with the flames around us, truth is refined as never before. We come to perceive and acknowledge who we really are. All this is part of what it means to lift up the soul.

Faith

For the psalmist, there is someone before whom to lift the soul. This entire psalm, in fact, is an act of extraordinary faith. Despite the experience of tears and struggle, despite being "lonely and afflicted" and surrounded by foes, the psalmist has the courage to trust that God will hear and respond.

Sometimes we are not so confident ourselves. We may indeed pray as the psalmist did, full of faith and hope, yet receive no answer. What does that tell us, either about God or about ourselves? What does Psalm 25 teach us for when that happens?

Actually, we do not know whether the psalmist's prayer was answered. But we do know when our own prayers are not. We must also admit that we are not always good at knowing when our prayers *are* answered.

Part of the problem lies in our expectations. The most common problem we have in relating to God is that we expect God to conform to our images, to function on our terms, and to accomplish our purposes. A lot of people would say that a God who does not do that is not a God worth following.

But there are still-wider possibilities for interpreting unanswered prayer. Prayers that are not visibly answered within a desired framework can be seen as signals for discipline and patience. They become promises of an answer that will come in due time and in the most appropriate way. From that perspective, unanswered prayers challenge the scope and orientation of our entire thinking process, inviting us to trust in a grander design for life. Sometimes the arranging of circumstances or the coming together of factors necessary for the best response takes time to accomplish.

Another way of understanding prayers thwarted is in terms of obstructing forces—evil, Satan, whatever name we choose to identify the contrary influences in life.

Whatever explanation we choose, we are left with some degree of uncertainty. For the nature of faith is to believe despite, beyond, and even in contrast to certainty. Faith, in that sense, transcends certainty. Still, many of our key prayers and hopes in life do go unfulfilled. Whether that says more about our capacity for dreaming, about the nature of life, or about a mystery we don't yet understand is for each of us to decide.

Choices

In the psalmist's case the choice was clear. The psalmist chose faith, whatever the outcome. Whether the psalmist had as many choices as we do today is unclear. But ultimately all of us, like the psalmist, choose faith in someone or something. What varies is the nature of that in which we place our trust. Trust in ourselves, trust in God, trust in those around us—all these are personal choices we make. The question is, what is the basis of our trust? According to what criteria and for what purposes do we choose the trusts we do?

For the psalmist a prior belief in the nature of God's love stood behind the decision to trust in God. It was God's promised goodness to which the psalmist appealed.

> Be mindful of thy mercy, O LORD,
>   and of thy steadfast love,
>   for they have been from of old. . . .
> According to thy steadfast love remember me,
>   for thy goodness' sake, O LORD!
>
> Psalm 25:6, 7b

In the psalmist's world-view the ultimate nature of reality was benevolent. The Creator was defined as merciful and loving. Consequently, the psalmist felt able to trust that love to enter and to empower the psalmist's own life, no matter how torn life became or how corrupted by failure.

As with the psalmist, how we understand life and the nature of ultimate reality will help us determine the choices we make and where we place our trust. When we examine the presuppositions of our beliefs, we discover the basic questions that face us.

The psalmist opted for love as the basis of the universe. In love was hope, both for personal deliverance and for the conclusion of all human history.

Change

This also meant that the psalmist was open to change, to learning. For hope has to do with deliverance, with a change of circumstances. It follows that one who dares hope dares change. The psalmist's openness to change appears in a willingness to be instructed in a new manner of life:

> Make me to know thy ways. . . .
> Lead me in thy truth and teach me.
>
> Psalm 25:4a, 5a

We sense here a sincere longing to remedy the mistakes of the past and to develop new patterns for more healthful and constructive living.

Perhaps we all have within us the basic desire to live rightly, to develop patterns of behavior that will enhance our happiness and our relationships in life. But like the psalmist, we so easily stray from proven paths and wander into dead ends. We, too, need to be reeducated as to what paths are most beneficial for our own lives.

Confession and Forgiveness

A critical component of this process of change and correction is confession. Three times in this psalm the writer confesses wrongdoing. There is an honest recognition of failure and helplessness accompanied by an earnest desire for forgiveness and renewal.

For all of us the power of confession needs to be clear. Confession is a tool by which we lay aside past mistakes. It cleanses the soul and prepares us for new possibilities. It is an act of honesty that enables trust to grow. When there are hidden agendas and undisclosed details that might resurface to damage relationships, and when energy must continually be expended to keep those secrets hidden, then our relationships are prevented from reaching their potential. Confession is essentially a means by which we make ourselves vulnerable to each other, and it is vulnerability, in turn, that enables us to be connected.

The corollary to confession is forgiveness. What the psalm writer's experience illustrates for us is that a large portion of healing has to do with forgiveness. Forgiveness is that liberating power that enables us to transcend the estrangements and conflicts of the past and to create new relationships. Forgiveness is what allows us to see ourselves and to be seen by others in new ways. It means that we need not be defined by our failures.

> Remember not the sins of my youth, . . .
> according to thy steadfast love remember me.
>
> Psalm 25:7a, b

Forgiveness is the act of seeing others graciously. This whole psalm, in fact, is an appeal to be seen graciously. The psalmist's experience has been to be measured not only by the consequences of personal guilt and failure but also by the standards of others that go way beyond what is appropriate for judgment.

That can be true for us as well. Already conscious of our guilt and failure, we have paid in our souls and lives a sufficient cost for the errors and wrongs of our own commission. But in the eyes of others we are penalized again and again and much more severely than is either necessary or helpful. Religious institutions, the supposed keepers of grace, are often the worst offenders in this arena.

Fortunately, the psalmist had a higher court of appeal. In full acknowledgment of failure, the psalmist recognized the need for amendment, but at the same time appealed for a just correction of the excessive opposition from others. While confessing personal culpability, the psalmist was also justified in calling down judgment on those whose opposition or hostility had gone too far.

Again, it is not that the psalmist was altogether innocent. When the psalm writer says, "May integrity and uprightness preserve me" (Ps 25:21a), it is not an integrity the psalmist already has, which can be banked as credit toward deliverance. Rather, it is an imputed integrity, given by grace.

Mercy

Behind this appeal is a vision of grace that manifests itself in love and mercy. In another verse the psalmist writes,

> Good and upright is the LORD;
> therefore [God] instructs sinners in the way.
>
> Psalm 25:8

This verse does not say, "God instructs the righteous." It says, "God instructs sinners." There is an implicit picture here not of rejection but of reconciliation. God is represented as one who, out of goodness and perfection, reaches out to help those who have failed and who ask for help.

Altogether, this psalm reflects a remarkably mature relationship between the writer and God. There is an intimacy, a closeness, that allows the free expression of guilt, anguish, longing, and, finally, trust.

These words make room for us to express the same kinds of feelings in our own lives. They give us space to acknowledge our guilt and to be freed from it. This psalm can help us to express the anguish we feel and to appeal not only for relief but for the curbing of those who unjustly accuse or oppress us. It also offers an image of learning, an openness to redirecting ourselves along more constructive paths.

Finally, the psalm models for us a world-view in which love and grace are available for redeeming our lives and restoring healthy relationships. It is a world-view of hope.

> Redeem Israel, O God,
> out of all [trouble].

Psalm 25:22

28

Patience and Change

I waited patiently for the LORD;
  [who] inclined to me and heard my cry.
[God] drew me up from the desolate pit,
  out of the miry bog,
and set my feet upon a rock,
  making my steps secure.
[God] put a new song in my mouth,
  a song of praise to our God.

Psalm 40:1-3a

I give thee thanks, O LORD, with my whole heart;
  before the gods I sing thy praise; . . .
  and give thanks to thy name
  for thy steadfast love and thy faithfulness; . . .
On the day I called, thou didst answer me,
  my strength of soul thou didst increase. . . .
Though I walk in the midst of trouble,
  thou dost preserve my life;
thou dost stretch out thy hand against the wrath of my
    enemies,
  and thy right hand delivers me.
The LORD will fulfill his purpose for me;
  thy steadfast love, O LORD, endures for ever.
  Do not forsake the work of thy hands.

Psalm 138:1, 2b, 3, 7-8

Patience pays. Deliverance is possible. Both of these psalms are testimonies to that.

For most of us patience does not come easily. By nature we are apt to desire speedy resolution to our problems and desires. That tendency is reinforced by life in a culture that caters to immediate personal gratification through everything from microwaveable meals to the promise of instant lottery wealth.

Patience requires a "letting go" mentality, an ability to lay aside not only our immediate inclinations but also the frustrations that go with them. To have patience is to yield control over current preferences in the faith that the desired outcome will eventually be won. Such letting go and yielding control is not particularly compatible with the prevailing cultural message to grab and control as much as we can as quickly as possible. Usually we come to patience only as a last resort, when it is forced upon us by a lack of alternatives.

But there is another dimension to patience that makes it seem less submissive. The truer essence of patience is perseverance—not a total giving up on a goal but rather the exact opposite, a tenacious expectation that the desired outcome will be accomplished in time. Patience in this light is a form of endurance. It is a manifestation of renewed commitment, as perhaps the psalmist was referring to:

> On the day I called, thou didst answer me,
> my strength of soul thou didst increase.
>
> Psalm 138:3

Sometimes it is suffering itself that strengthens the soul and develops patience, though the process whereby that is accomplished is painful and the strength gained is usually not fully appreciated until the suffering is past.

The trick is to know what merits our hard-won patience, what dreams or conditions are worth the wait or the cost. Too often we spend our patience on desires that are transient or of lesser quality than we deserve, whether in relationships, career accomplishments, or material gain. True wisdom includes the ability to discern those goals that patience best serves. It also includes the ability to know when to wait patiently and when to energetically pursue that which we desire.

Fulfillment

What the psalm writers tell us is that the deliverance for which they waited actually came. It was not just a pipe dream on which they expended their hope. Their dreams had concrete results. When the psalmists spoke of their own waiting and encouraged others to learn how to wait as well, it was with a conviction born of experience.

> For God alone my soul waits in silence;
>> from [God] comes my salvation.
>
> Psalm 62:1

> I wait for the LORD, my soul waits,
>> and in [God's] word I hope. . . .
> For with the LORD there is steadfast love,
>> and with [God] is plenteous redemption.
>
> Psalm 130:5, 7

> Wait for the LORD;
>> be strong, and let your heart take courage.
>
> Psalm 27:14a, b

When the strength that comes through suffering is combined with the testimony of others that hopes really can be realized through courageous waiting, then patience becomes more appealing as an approach to the great frustrations of our lives. To actualize that patience, however, we need to cling to the stories of those who have already been delivered.

The psalmists record for us a glimpse of life beyond the Pit. Their claim is that with external help, ways can indeed be found out of the miry bog of our lives. We, like they, can be led by stepping stones out of the swamp to solid rocks upon which to find secure footing.

> [God] drew me up from the desolate pit,
>> out of the miry bog,
> and set my feet upon a rock,
>> making my steps secure.

[God] put a new song in my mouth,
 a song of praise to our God.

Psalm 40:2-3a

After spending so much of life on slippery ledges and fighting through the mud and muck of our lives, this image of solid ground has powerful appeal. So, too, does the news of a fresh song to sing once the bog is behind us. At times, we would be grateful to feel any song at all, so barren does our soul become. The old dirges become too dreary and empty to sustain us.

Both of these psalms portray actual experiences of deliverance. They tell of enemies defeated or at least held at arm's length, thanks to the steadfast love and grace that underlie life.

What the psalms also tell us, however, is that deliverance may not be total in the sense that enemies will be permanently obliterated. Instead, deliverance may be a kind of space created in the midst of life's continuing troubles to help us regain our composure and confidence for pressing on.

Though I walk in the midst of trouble,
 thou dost preserve my life.

Psalm 138:7a

In this case the trouble is a continuing reality, but it is no longer a defeating reality. The threat of annihilation is overcome. Thus we see that in Psalm 40, the writer goes from giving thanks for deliverance from one bog to appealing for help out of another.

Persistence for a Purpose

Unfortunately, deliverance may not be a permanent state. After surviving and growing through one set of obstacles, we often encounter others. Hopefully, few of us will face more than a handful of major crises in our lives. Some may experience only one or two. But it would be naive to expect none at all. It is a characteristic of human life and growth that we are assaulted by great difficulties from time to time. They may be of our own making or of someone else's or even the product of wider social turmoil. However they come, they test us, sometimes to the limit.

To endure, survive, and profit from them, we need to hold on to those promises and examples that others have passed on to us from their own battles. The psalms include a series of such messages. They tell us of life preserved, and because life is something we value so highly, it is good news indeed that it can be preserved, enhanced, and redeemed.

But the psalms offer more than messages of survival and encouragement. They also speak of purpose: "The LORD will fulfill his purpose for me" (Ps 138:8a).

To believe that one has a purpose in life works wonders. It enables us to accomplish extraordinary deeds. It satisfies our longing for meaning. It provides us with a sense of value, so necessary for self-esteem, healthy relationships, and a productive life.

One modern hymn, which describes us as love's own creation, provides an almost psalm-like affirmation that we all have a special purpose, despite life's traumas and trials.

> Amid the world's bleak wilderness
> A vineyard grows with promise green,
> The planting of the Lord himself.
>
> His love selected this terrain;
> His vine with love he planted here
> To bear the choicest fruit for him.
>
> We are his branches, chosen, dear,
> And though we feel the dresser's knife,
> We are the objects of his care.
>
> From him we draw the juice of life,
> For him supply his winery
> With fruit from which true joys derive.
>
> Vine, keep what I was meant to be:
> Your branch, with your rich life in me.
>
> Jaroslav J. Vajda*

*Text copyright © 1978 *Lutheran Book of Worship*. Stanzas 1–5 reproduced by permission of Augsburg Fortress. Hymn title: "Amid the World's Bleak Wilderness"; tune by Richard Hillert.

The psalmists describe our value in a variety of ways. "Do not forsake the work of thy hands" (Ps 138:8b), writes one. Contained in these words is a sense of value and identity based on a particular relationship. The psalmist can claim worth based on the stake God has in creation. As God stands for all that is ultimate, eternal, and perfect, so must we, the offspring of God's creative power, implicitly be valuable. Elsewhere, other psalmists explicitly marvel at the amazing value and significance with which God has imbued humankind (e.g., Ps 8).

What is implicit in this concept is that we discover our value primarily through relationship. Each person has value as an individual, but that value has meaning only in the context of human community.

Our value is expressed in yet another way:

> As for me, I am poor and needy;
> but the Lord takes thought for me.
>
> Psalm 40:17a

That there are those who would "take thought for us" in life is a lovely idea, all the more so when one of those is the Master of all life. At a deep level, all of us need to know that our existence is noticed and valued, especially in moments of weakness and vulnerability. To be cared about is proof of the value we long to have.

Gratitude

There is yet one more aspect of these psalms that reveals for us the wider meaning of deliverance. Here, as elsewhere in the psalms, the experience of deliverance issues forth in thanksgiving and public testimony:

> I give thee thanks, O LORD, with my whole heart;
> before the gods I sing thy praise.
>
> Psalm 138:1

> Many will see and fear,
> and put their trust in the LORD. . . .

I have told the glad news of deliverance
  in the great congregation;
lo, I have not restrained my lips,
  as thou knowest, O LORD.
I have not hid thy saving help within my heart.

Psalm 40:3b, 9-10a

Public recounting of deliverance seems to follow as a necessary corollary to the experience itself. Several factors may account for that. First, there is the swell of relief and the burst of joy that follows a dramatic deliverance. The emotions that accompany such an experience cannot be contained.

Secondly, there may—rightfully—be a sense of obligation, a debt of gratitude to the ones who have enabled our rescue. A demonstration of appreciation is entirely appropriate.

In times of crisis, we often make promises. To fulfill these when the crisis is past is to keep faith not only with others but with ourself.

Finally, the expressions of gratitude, the fulfillment of vows, and the public testimonies to deliverance are vehicles for establishing a new set of relationships through which we reconnect to others in constructive and creative new ways. These acts signal the positive changes we intend to make in our lives outside the Pit.

Deliverance and change go together. These psalms show us that both are truly possible.

29

Love, Thanksgiving, and Dreams

> *I love the LORD, because [God] has heard*
> *my voice and my supplications.*
> *Because [God has listened] to me,*
> *. . . I will call on [God] as long as I live.*
> *The snares of death encompassed me;*
> *the pangs of Sheol laid hold on me;*
> *I suffered distress and anguish.*
> *Then I called on the name of the LORD:*
> *"O LORD, I beseech thee, save my life!"*
> *Gracious is the LORD, and righteous;*
> *our God is merciful.*
> *The LORD preserves the simple;*
> *when I was brought low, [God] saved me.*
> *Return, O my soul, to your rest;*
> *for the LORD has dealt bountifully with you.*
> *For thou hast delivered my soul from death,*
> *my eyes from tears,*
> *my feet from stumbling;*
> *I walk before the LORD*
> *in the land of the living.*

Psalm 116:1-11

This psalm portrays a powerful experience of deliverance. In this account we see the effect deliverance can have.

Love and Regeneration

> I love the LORD, because [God] has heard
> my voice and my supplications.

Psalm 116:1

The first thing we notice is that deliverance releases love. When we have experienced great love and grace, we are inspired to return it. Deliverance renews our capacity to reengage with the life-forces around us. In an awesome way, it carries its own regenerative power, as it triggers the impulse to reconnect with those who have been instrumental in our liberation and to make new connections with others who come into our lives. It frees us to respond to those who have responded to us in our time of trial and to form new attachments. For love inspires love. As we have known love, so are we empowered to transmit it.

Sometimes that transmission process is blocked. If we have not known love ourselves, if love has been blocked by critical, demeaning messages or by the message that love itself is weak, immature, or a waste of time, then our life will be shorted out in ways that will leave us deeply dissatisfied. For love is an energy. It needs to flow through us without interruption to make the appliances of life work—the relationships, the labors, even the pleasures. When the current of love is cut off, whole areas of our life are blacked out. We stumble in dark corners and wander in dim passages until the energy is turned on again. Deliverance is like someone throwing the switch. It is a new source of light-shedding power.

This renewal is what the psalmist experienced after a period of wandering in dim passages. Clearly, there is no doubt that the psalm writer's experience of darkness was genuine. The being brought low, the tears and the stumbling that come when life is out of balance, these are testimonies to a life deeply touched by suffering. Such a life is a trustworthy witness when it announces deliverance.

Death and Deliverance

Just how powerful an effect this experience of deliverance had is glimpsed in a reference to what would have happened if death had actually come:

> Precious in the sight of the LORD
> is the death of his saints.
>
> Psalm 116:15

How can we call death precious? What kind of experience can be so powerful that it relativizes even death? Obviously the author of this psalm had been so profoundly moved by the combination of suffering, survival, and deliverance that death itself had lost its threat. Life had been cast in completely new terms. The psalmist was so filled with confidence and a new vision that old fears were transcended.

This had not been an automatic transition. There had been a period when the psalmist lost faith in friends, gave up hope in official appeals, and was generally disappointed in the ability of neighbors to help.

> I said in my consternation,
>   "[People] are all a vain hope."
>
> Psalm 116:11

But throughout these ordeals, the psalmist kept faith with deep, personal convictions. Even when there were reasons to doubt that any transcendent assistance would come, the psalmist held true to this basic belief.

> I kept my faith, even when I said,
>   "I am greatly afflicted."
>
> Psalm 116:10

The result was worth it. What the psalmist came to experience was a new and satisfying sense of peace, expressed beautifully in the phrase, "Return, O my soul, to your rest" (Ps 116:7a).

What this wistfully suggests is that life should naturally contain some spheres or periods of peace, that we do indeed deserve to have places and times when our soul can know rest. Clearly, the psalmist found such stability and refreshment. To speak of walking "in the land of the living" conveys a profound appreciation for the gift of life. It is an appreciation born out of firsthand experience with the obliterating implications of death.

We know how that feels. When we get a second chance, an opportunity for a fresh start, it can feel like a return to "the land of the living." As we enter that land, a new burst of energy rises in our soul. We walk erect again, nourished in spirit by gratitude and a healed self-image.

Thanksgiving

But simply being free again isn't enough. We remain incomplete until we respond to our deliverance in ways that will keep us connected to it. The psalmist expressed it with a question and a response:

> What shall I render to the LORD
>   for all [God's] bounty to me?
> I will lift up the cup of salvation
>   and call on the name of the LORD, . . .
> I will pay my vows to the LORD
>   in the presence of all [God's] people,
> in the courts of the house of the LORD,
>   in your midst, O Jerusalem.
>
> Psalm 116:12-13, 18-19

After experiencing such deliverance, the psalmist could not just walk away and forget it. To do so would have cheapened the experience. It might also have opened the psalmist to repeating the experience of suffering by forgetting which paths led to it in the first place. We need to hold on to the memory of our deliverance, if we hope to avoid a return to the Pit.

Then too, there is a sense of gratitude we need to express, and a healthy sense of obligation. This kind of healthy obligation is a tool for reconnecting with others, and it serves to bind us together in mutual support. It is a sign of the positive valuing of self and of others.

After experiencing such a great deliverance, the psalmist knew that no one-shot, simple token of appreciation would be sufficient to express the joy and the value of the experience. What had been gained was more than could ever be repaid. What's more, the act of repayment and thanksgiving was no burden. It would be, instead, a way of keeping alive the memory of deliverance and of cultivating the new perspectives that had been won. Ultimately, it was as much an act of self-affirmation as an expression of gratitude.

What that illustrates for us is that our recovery and health have a great deal to do with retaining a focus outside ourselves. By connecting with a community through our testimony of deliverance and through our acts of giving thanks, we expand, enrich, and protect our recovered self. It was no accident that the psalmist named a community in which to express thanks and to offer service. It was a deliberate choice, meant to preserve the meaning of deliverance.

In the community the psalmist found security and a place to grow. There the psalmist could serve and help others in ways that might even contribute to their deliverance. There, too, the psalmist was able to keep self in perspective and ego under control, as witnessed in the words,

> O LORD, I am thy servant;
> I am thy servant, the [child] of thy handmaid.
>
> Psalm 116:16

Humility

In these words we see not only the humility of the psalmist in relation to God but also the wider recognition that no one is a self-created, independent being. We all come from somewhere. And we all have our limits. To find peace in life, one of the first steps is to give up our delusions of grandeur and superiority—born of our fears and insecurities—and to develop instead a healthy perspective about who we are in relation to those around us. For the more clearly we discover our complete identity, the freer we will be to develop and enjoy it. What we will discover along the way, much to our delight, is that, increasingly, others will affirm and support us, too. For humility, which is essentially a mature understanding of the nature of our relationships, frees others from their fears and insecurities as well. That, in turn, allows them to engage more deeply and positively with us.

So, in turning to a community in response to deliverance, the psalmist was developing those resources that would ultimately be to the psalmist's own benefit. There the psalmist could keep alive the good memories of deliverance and also the useful memories of what is to be avoided and why. In community the psalmist could find the support and balanced self-understanding that could lead to long-term satisfaction.

Jerusalems

The psalmist also found a stable center, an external symbol of purpose and direction "in your midst, O Jerusalem." Jerusalem symbolized a reality larger, longer lasting, and more constant than the content of any individual life with all its up's and down's. In the image of Jerusalem the psalmist found a timeless treasure of meaning and motivation for the days and years ahead. Jerusalem was a place of dreams, a calling toward the future, a promise of well-being and fulfillment.

Whatever our Jerusalem might be, it is important that we envision such a place. For we all need such magnificent, rich symbols of hope and purpose. They give us direction in life. They are places from which we derive and strengthen our identity. They provide stable reference points and a meeting place for connecting with fellow travelers. To have a Jerusalem is to have both a dream and the inspiration to follow it. In our Jerusalems we find our past and our future. Our dreams of Jerusalem are what make deliverance worthwhile.

30

The Cadence of Hope

O give thanks to the LORD, *for [God] is good;*
  [God's] steadfast love endures for ever!
Let the redeemed of the LORD *say so,*
  whom [God] has redeemed from trouble. . . .
Some wandered in desert wastes, . . .
hungry and thirsty,
  their soul fainted within them.
Then they cried to the LORD *in their trouble,*
  and [God] delivered them from their distress. . . .
Some sat in darkness and in gloom,
  prisoners in affliction and in irons,
for they had rebelled against the words of God. . . .
Their hearts were bowed down. . . .
Then they cried to the LORD *in their trouble,*
  and [God] delivered them from their distress. . . .
Some were sick through their sinful ways,
  and because of their iniquities suffered affliction. . . .
Then they cried to the LORD *in their trouble,*
  and [God] delivered them from their distress. . . .
Some went down to the sea in ships,
  doing business on the great waters. . . .
They mounted up to heaven, they went down to the depths;
  their courage melted away in their evil plight;
they reeled and staggered like drunken men,
  and were at their wits' end.
Then they cried to the LORD *in their trouble,*
  and [God] delivered them from their distress. . . .

Let them thank the LORD for [this] steadfast love,
for [God's] wonderful works to [humankind]!
Whoever is wise, . . . give heed to these things;
let [all] consider the steadfast love of the LORD.
                                    Psalm 107:1-2, 4-6, 10-11a, 12a, 13,
                                            17, 19, 23, 26-28, 31, 43

It beats like a cadence throughout this psalm. It echoes time and again from one psalm to another, no matter what the circumstances. It permeates the whole of life as the psalmists come to know it:

O give thanks to the LORD, for [God] is good;
[God's] steadfast love endures for ever!
                                                    Psalm 107:1

Goodness and love—these are the code words of reality, as one psalm writer after another found to be true. Over and over the psalmists testify to the power of love. To this love they appeal when other resources are exhausted, even when they know that they have no justification in their own lives for what they ask. "The steadfast love of the Lord" is the shaping reality of the psalmists' dreams.

Love's Seed

At times, however, that love seemed distant. The psalm writers went through periods of deep emptiness and despair. At times, love's power was more an anguished last grasping than a close, tangible reality.

But somewhere within the writers' souls there was yet enough of life's breath to voice one further appeal. It was an appeal that made sense only because such grace and love had already been tasted, at least in some small way. Love's seed itself had been planted in the psalmists' hearts, and enough of it remained to give rise to their vision of deliverance.

So it is with us. Somewhere in our souls there is an ancient experience of love. There is the faint, throbbing sense that life can have hope. Somewhere inside us the lingering taste of love gives birth to our own restless longing for deliverance. If we did not hold in the heart of our soul this soft rhythm of love, we could not envision its realization in our lives. Life would be only dreary, without color. But the dream does lie within, and with it we find our redemption.

> Then they cried to the LORD in their trouble,
> and God delivered them from their distress.
>
> Psalm 107:6, 13, 19, 28

The power of love is the power to deliver. Love is the heart that listens to our cries and responds to our distress.

To know that we have a place to carry our cries is itself a tremendous relief. In the image of One who hears and cares we find comfort, aware that we are not alone in this boundless universe. There is One to whom our existence matters.

Given the pervasive brokenness of life, we need such assurance. For the cries will come, abundantly, repeatedly, painfully, and in a multitude of ways.

Desert Places

One of the images the psalmist chose for the reality of brokenness was the image of wandering in desert places:

> Some wandered in desert wastes,
> finding no way to a city to dwell in;
> hungry and thristy,
> their soul fainted within them.
> Then they cried to the LORD, . . .
> God led them by a straight way,
> till they reached a city to dwell in.
>
> Psalm 107:4–6a, 7

At times our lives, too, become barren. We know the scorching heat that sucks life dry, the irritating sands of frustration that clog and hinder our progress. We, too, have cast our gaze over troubles that resemble distant and endless desert landscapes, littered with thorny and jagged obstacles that threaten us. We know what it is like to stand exposed to the searing blasts of our accusers, unable to find shelter or a path out of the wilderness.

No wonder our souls faint. Like those souls in the psalm, there are so many things for which we hunger and thirst—peace, companionship, joy, refreshment, a secure place in which to dwell.

The psalmist's image of deliverance is of receiving exactly what we desire: a direct path out of our desert places. Instead of being left in the desert, we are guided to a place of refuge.

For the psalmist a city serves as the symbol of protection, of refreshment, and of the resources we need to recover from our wanderings. The city represents life. It is an opportunity for revival and fresh beginnings.

The city is also the place of community. In the desert we are usually alone. While there may be people with us sharing the suffering, the truth is that they too may be lost. In the city we can be reconnected with a wider community, one that is able to respect our suffering yet lead us beyond it.

But the desert is only one of the places in which we get lost. Besides the private wildernesses of our lives there are also the areas we share with others. Here, too, the psalmist speaks of deliverance, in this case using the sea with its wonders and dangers as a symbol of ordinary life:

> Some went down to the sea in ships,
>   doing business on the great waters;
> they saw the deeds of the LORD,
>   God's wondrous works in the deep.
> For God commanded, and raised the stormy wind,
>   which lifted up the waves of the sea. . . .
>   Their courage melted away . . . ;
>   they were at their wits' end.
> Then they cried to the LORD . . .
>   and [God] delivered them from their distress;
> [God] made the storm be still,
>   and the waves of the sea were hushed.
> Then they were glad because they had quiet,
>   and [God] brought them to their desired haven.
>
> Psalm 107:23-25, 26b, 27b, 28-30

We often get swamped by the storms of life. We go about our regular business, unaware of the brewing maelstroms. Sometimes it does not take much to upset our routine or to dispel our composure. But when the truly big waves come smashing in, then it is that we realize how vulnerable and powerless we are.

Nature is a good teacher of proportion. As a storm at sea can sink a ship, as a tornado on land can level a town, so can the disasters that sweep over our lives and relationships prove incredibly devastating. Nature unleashed can destroy everything we know, including life itself. Nothing so reminds us of our insignificance in the cosmos as standing before the results of nature's wrath. Likewise, the devastations wrought by human failure and conflict remind us of our need to consider our finitude, to recover a sense of proportion in the way we live and relate to others.

> Whoever is wise, . . . give heed to these things;
> let [all] consider the steadfast love of the LORD.
>
> Psalm 107:43

Wisdom and Self-Denial

Wisdom calls us to look beyond ourselves, and to connect with those things that are more stable and constant than we are. To be wise is to deliberately and thoughtfully turn one's life toward those commitments and activities that are the most constructive, not only for ourselves but also for those with whom we share this existence.

> And let them offer sacrifices of thanksgiving,
> and tell of [God's] deeds in songs of joy!
>
> Psalm 107:22

There is in this verse a call to sacrificial living, the kind that acknowledges our relationships as well as our responsibility to demonstrate our interdependence through acts of self-denial. To withhold our self-giving, to hold on to the illusion that we are totally independent beings with no need to be vulnerable to others, is a path back to destruction and emptiness.

The joy in this verse is connected to communication, which means involvement with other people in mutual sharing and self-giving. An implication of that connectedness is that while a sacrificial lifestyle is beneficial to ourselves, it may also aid others in their passage through life's seas.

Boundless Grace

One point this psalm makes is that there is no circumstance in which deliverance can not come. No one can be so lost in any desert, so tossed on any sea, so imprisoned by any failing, or so devastated by any affliction that hope is completely lost. Even when we have violated all justice and morality, rebelled against common sense and social responsibilities—no matter what we have done to others or to ourselves—it is the psalmist's testimony that deliverance waits for those who can admit their need and see beyond it:

> Then they cried to the LORD in their trouble,
>   and [God] delivered them from their distress;
> [God] brought them out of darkness and gloom,
>   and broke their bonds asunder. . . .
> [God] sent forth his word, and healed them,
>   and delivered them from destruction.
> Let them thank the LORD for [this] steadfast love,
>   for [God's] wonderful works to [humankind]!
>
> Psalm 107:13-14, 20-21

There is no limit to this deliverance that awaits us. It is as comprehensive as the sins we are able to commit.

> Let the redeemed of the LORD say so,
>   whom [God] has redeemed from trouble
> and gathered in from the lands,
>   from the east and from the west,
>   from the north and from the south.
>
> Psalm 107:2-3

It was the experience of the psalm writers that the scope of deliverance was boundless. The love of this Lord in whom they trusted was as universal as human wandering. There was no place it could not reach and redeem.

This is not to suggest that deliverance is either automatic or cheap. It comes with a serious call to respond in thanksgiving, sacrificial self-opening, and a free sharing of our joy—all of which connect us more closely with those around us. It is a call to community and to service with and for others.

But that is not strange—the psalms themselves were products of the lives of individuals in community and were preserved by the communities who heard and found them valuable. Now they are offered to us, both as individuals and as members of the communities from which we come and in which we live our lives.

In the end as in the beginning, life is a relational affair. And only in relationship can love be engaged. The love that brings deliverance comes not from a vacuum; rather, it is the active flowering of our engagement with a reality greater than ourselves, a reality channeled one way or another through community.

> Whoever is wise, . . . give heed to these things;
> let [all] consider the steadfast love of the LORD.
>
> Psalm 107:43

31

Blessing

Bless the LORD, O my soul;
  and all that is within me, bless his holy name!
Bless the LORD, O my soul,
  and forget not all his benefits,
who forgives all your iniquity,
  who heals all your diseases,
who redeems your life from the Pit,
  who crowns you with steadfast love and mercy,
who satisfies you with good as long as you live
  so that your youth is renewed like the eagle's.
The LORD works vindication and
  justice for all who are oppressed.
He made known his ways to Moses,
  his acts to the people of Israel.
The LORD is merciful and gracious,
  slow to anger and abounding in steadfast love.
He will not always chide,
  nor will he keep his anger for ever.
He does not deal with us according to our sins,
  nor requite us according to our iniquities.
For as the heavens are high above the earth,
  so great is his steadfast love toward those who fear him;
as far as the east is from the west,
  so far does he remove our transgressions from us.
As a father pities his children,
  so the LORD pities those who fear him.

> *For he knows our frame;*
> *he remembers that we are dust.*

> Psalm 103:1-14

Most psalms of deliverance use past-tense verbs:

> I love the LORD, because he *has heard*
> my voice and my supplications. . . .
> When I was brought low, he *saved* me. . . .
> *For thou hast delivered* my soul from death.

> Psalm 116:1, 6b, 8a (italics added)

> I *waited* aptiently for the LORD;
> he *inclined* to me and *heard* my cry.

> Psalm 40:1 (italics added)

Those past-tense verbs are shouts of joy. They are stories of deliverance accomplished. They speak of suffering ended, of times of trial that are over. They celebrate the change from oppression to deliverance.

In contrast, the verbs of Psalm 103 are predominantly present and future tense. They portray a continuing reality instead of a one-time transition, and their message is even more powerful and comforting than the news of a specific deliverance. For what these present-tense verbs convey is a sense of continuing deliverance, future as well as present. In faith they proclaim that the power of deliverance will ultimately triumph over the powers of destruction.

Blessing Mentality

Out of such confidence is born a powerful new vision. Call it the "blessing mentality," that attitude that focuses on what may be affirmed and celebrated. It is born of the wisdom that perceives life as gift, not burden.

The blessing mentality can arise even without a particularly dramatic experience of deliverance. It emerges when the cursing mentality has passed, when we are ready to move beyond the darkness of our pain into the light of new promise. The blessing mentality affirms life. It affirms self, others, relationships, and even what has been learned from the times of devastation and cursing.

It reflects a new set of choices we have made, a new orientation toward that which is life-giving and life-sustaining, both for ourselves and for others. The orientation of Psalm 103, for example, is not simply to recount and give thanks for one individual's deliverance. It is also meant to encourage others by proclaiming and modeling the reliable grounds for hoping in deliverance.

The blessing mentality is a declaration of intent. It is a commitment of our whole being to a proper acknowledgment of our status as vulnerable, fallible, transient creatures who yet may find love and deliverance given to us, not because we deserve it but because there is a greater love that surrounds our lives. It is to this greater love that we open our souls, confessing our brokenness and receiving healing in return. ". . . all that is within me, bless his holy name!" (Ps 103:1b).

In that sense, the blessing mentality is a declaration not of independence, not of self-sufficiency, not of our own desire for godhood. Rather, it is a declaration of healthy dependence, of a life committed to living in healing relationships during the days available to us.

> As for man, his days are like grass;
>   he flourishes like a flower of the field;
> for the wind passes over it, and it is gone,
>   and its place knows it no more.
> But the steadfast love of the LORD
> is from everlasting to everlasting
>   upon those who fear him, . . .
> to those who keep his covenant.
>
> Psalm 103:15-17a, 18a

We may indeed be transient. Our lives may be brief and often broken. But the love that guides this universe can imbue our lives with a quality that transcends time and transience. In this relationship with love lies the power to supersede the narrow boundaries of our immediate mortal being and to connect us with a wonder that lasts forever.

Gifts

The blessing mentality understands this potential. Consequently, it does not miss or minimize the gifts of life.

> Bless the LORD, O my soul,
>   and forget not all his benefits.
>
> Psalm 103:2

To focus on life's benefits—to count our blessings, so to speak—serves two purposes. It helps us cultivate a sense of gratitude, which is none other than a necessary sense of perspective. And it helps us not only to counteract negative influences in our lives but to develop a capacity for concentrating our energies on positive possibilities.

The most positive possibility of all and that upon which the blessing mentality is based is the one presented in the Psalm, namely, that our failures and hurts can be completely mended by One

> who forgives all your iniquity,
>   who heals all your diseases.
>
> Psalm 103:2

The power of this remarkable claim lies in its completeness. There is a sense of totality here. In the little word "all" is contained the extraordinary suggestion that everything we have ever done wrong can be completely erased, that every hurt we have ever felt can be completely healed.

Normally, our best hope when failure or injury or iniquity has surfaced in our lives is that such disturbances will eventually fade. What we seek is recovery from the effects of our wrongdoings or the wrong done to us.

But what the psalmist shows us and what Scripture pledges elsewhere is that our failures can not only be forgiven but actually forgotten. And the remarkable assertion of the psalmist is that *all* our failures can be forgiven; *all* our brokenness can be healed. There is no aspect of our lives, no flaw in our character, no deed we have done, that cannot be overwhelmed, expunged, and offset by the power of grace.

That is the good news pervading all Scripture. That is the vision behind this psalm. That is the promise held by faith. And that is what most of us long for above all else as we suffer the effects of life's brokenness. We ache to be set free, to be clean again, to be healed of the injuries life brings. Whether our wounds have been caused by the malice, the negligence, or the ignorance of others, or whether our own conscience bears the heavy burden of having created our broken condition, what we long for is deliverance. What our spirit desires is release from oppression, freedom from judgment, and an end to the anger, sorrow, and shame we have known.

Compassion

John Baillie in his marvelous devotional book *A Diary of Private Prayer* includes a petition for "those who are suffering the consequences of misdeeds long ago repented of."* This lovely, sensitive prayer reflects the same spirit of grace as that recorded in the psalm. It mirrors the compassion of divine forgiveness.

The divine approach to human brokenness is to forgive and to heal, especially once the brokenness is confessed. When the wounded heart has repented and when that contrition begins to unfold in the lives of those who have suffered brokenness and its consequences, then it is the divine decision that the sentence has been served. Grace grants the freedom to begin anew.

Human judgment, however, often differs. In our hardness and fear, in our awareness of our own fundamental untrustworthiness, we resist granting trust to others. We are reluctant to set them free, to release them from the punishment we believe they deserve or which, perhaps, we sense that we may deserve ourselves, albeit for some other, undiscovered sin. It is as though by inflicting punishment on others, we can keep it at a distance from ourselves. The sentences we pronounce are often actually our attempts to set

*John Baillie, *A Diary of Private Prayer* (New York: Charles Scribner's Sons, 1949) 47.

boundaries around the chaos and imperfection that seethe within us all.

Forgiveness

True forgiveness is one of the hardest lessons for human beings to learn. It is the capacity to forgive perhaps that distinguishes human and divine. To truly forgive ourselves and those who have hurt us may in fact be the greatest challenge to the human spirit. To accomplish it takes a love akin to the divine, a love that expands the spirit beyond all ordinary experience. Scripture's testimony is that in such love lies salvation. Forgiveness expressed in love generates a power that can create profound new possibilities for all our relationships.

That is why the psalmist's words are so uplifting to the soul. They pronounce forgiveness in the very ways that we most long to hear it.

> Bless the Lord . . .
> who redeems your life from the Pit,
>   who crowns you with steadfast love and mercy,
> who satisfies you with good as long as you live
>   so that your youth is renewed like the eagle's.
> He will not always chide,
>   nor will he keep his anger for ever.
>
> Psalm 103:3a, 4, 5, 9

Who among us does not want our life redeemed? Who does not want to be overwhelmed by love? Who would not want to be released from anger and judgment? The very nature of hope is that our condition will improve, that the forces arrayed against us will be overcome, that our lives will be restored and purified.

The psalm's promise is that the chiding will end, that the anger will pass, that there is a limit to what we will have to endure. Unfortunately, human limits are seldom as gracious as God's. We may know our repentance and have full conviction of our forgiveness, yet we may have to endure the animosity of those who have not yet comprehended grace. The divine anger may pass and the debt be considered paid. Yet there are those around us whose anger and chiding will continue undiminished.

The tragedy then becomes theirs as much as ours. We may pray deliverance for ourselves, but deliverance remains the need of our accuser as well. Only when both are delivered is salvation complete.

Meanwhile, we need to avoid letting our accusers' problems cloud our own free conscience. One way to do that is to pray that someone else might see them as graciously as we ourselves have been seen. For when they, too, have been crowned with love and mercy, they may learn both forgiveness and how to give it. In time, we ourselves may become instruments of the grace they need.

Obstacles

That is not to say, however, that the path will be smooth or quick, though one could get that impression from the psalm. We know too well that even once delivered, we are not subsequently "satisfied with good as long as we live." Is the psalm then misleading? Are its promises of goodness, justice, and vindication empty?

It helps to know that the text itself is uncertain. The phrase "satisfies you with good as long as you live" is a provisional translation of the ancient Hebrew. The original meaning is unclear.

So, too, is life, as we know so well. The God referred to in Scripture clearly does not make our lives all good or work vindication and justice for all who are oppressed, at least not in one lifetime or according to our common perspectives. Inevitably, we are left with the question, "Why not?" Why does this God not impose justice and vindication as we expect and desire? Is it that our standards are too high, our expectations unrealistic? No, for these values themselves derive from our relationship to the divine. They are the same values this very God has taught us to hold.

How then are we to understand injustice, oppression, and suffering? Why does God not act?

Suffering

Over the centuries libraries have been filled and religions developed to explore such questions, for to penetrate the mystery of suffering is a deep drive of the human spirit.

The psalm does not seek to provide a simple answer. But it does offer clues for getting on with life while we ask the question.

> He made known his ways to Moses,
>   his acts to the people of Israel.
> The LORD is merciful and gracious,
>   slow to anger and abounding in steadfast love.
>
> Psalm 103:7-8

The psalmist points to what we do know based on personal experience and belief. First, the psalmist refers to historical precedent—those actions in the life of the believing community that illustrate divine intention and power. From that record, the psalmist suggests, we can be confirmed in our belief that history is indeed headed toward the establishment of justice and liberation by a God committed to both.

Then the psalmist appeals to the very nature of the divine as grounds for assurance. A God who is "slow to anger" and abounding in a steady, persistent love should be tremendously encouraging to anyone looking for comfort in the midst of life's trials.

We mortals are so easily moved to anger, so quick to take offense. Our love is so often fickle and self-serving. It is not surprising, then, that when we face trials or suffering, our weaknesses prevail and we are quickly distraught. In contrast, the God of the psalms represents consistency, patience, and a supremely positive power that can prevail over whatever trials life brings.

These are the responses the psalmist makes to the reality of life's suffering. We surely will continue to suffer from the faults and foibles of human nature and the conflicts and injustice they will continue to create. But beyond what is human is this boundless grace and deliverance. The good news of the psalm is that grace can operate even in the midst of human failure. No matter how badly we fail or are abused by others, there is a deliverance that can liberate us from our suffering.

As far as the east is from the west,
  so far does he remove our transgressions from us.
As a father pities his children,
  so the LORD pities those who fear him.
For he knows our frame;
  he remembers that we are dust.

Psalm 103:12-14

What more graphic and tender image can there be to comfort and encourage us as we face life's turmoil? In this image we find a love that understands us, compassion for our vulnerability, and a power at work to remove us from the consequences of our brokenness. As described in the New Testament (2 Cor 5:17) the picture here suggested is of a life so new, so different from what we have known, that when we receive it we may be justly called a "new creation." With such deliverance our spirit may be reborn in a new image of what it is to be human.

The psalmist does not say that such deliverance is free. It comes at the cost of our pain being absorbed into the heart of another. God, as it were, hurts for us. In turn, this deliverance calls forth from us a renewed commitment to an amended life lived out in a covenant of love, trust, faithfulness, mercy, and justice. That life is best nurtured in a community where we can continue to discover and be sustained by the overwhelming love the psalmist describes, the love that is able to make all things new.

32

From Tragedy to Redemption

Have mercy on me, O God, according to thy steadfast love;
  according to thy abundant mercy blot out my transgressions.
Wash me thoroughly from my iniquity,
  and cleanse me from my sin!
For I know my transgressions,
  and my sin is ever before me.
Against thee, thee only, have I sinned, . . .
  so that thou art justified in thy sentence. . . .
Behold, thou desirest truth in the inward being;
  therefore teach me wisdom in my secret heart.
Purge me with hyssop, and I shall be clean;
  wash me, and I shall be whiter than snow.
Fill me with joy and gladness;
  let the bones which thou hast broken rejoice.
Hide thy face from my sins,
  and blot out all my iniquities.
Create in me a clean heart, O God,
  and put a new and right spirit within me.
Cast me not away from thy presence,
  and take not thy holy Spirit from me.
Restore me to the joy of thy salvation,
  and uphold me with a willing spirit.
Then I will teach transgressors thy ways,
  and sinners will return to thee. . . .
O Lord, open thou my lips,
  and my mouth shall show forth thy praise. . . .
The sacrifice acceptable to God is a broken spirit;
a broken and contrite heart, O God, thou wilt not despise.

Psalm 51:1-3, 4a, b, 6-13, 15, 17

One might expect this psalm to be associated with a discussion about failure, corruption, repentance, and punishment. It is a classic expression of human remorse. Behind it lies a dramatic story of murder, adultery, abuse of power, and the most ugly kind of human duplicity.

Yet this psalm, as we shall soon see, forms part of a stunning story of deliverance. It belongs to one of the boldest statements in all of Scripture about the power of redemption and the possibility for new life.

The actual deliverance story is told in 2 Samuel 11–12. There we read how David, the great king of Israel, succumbed to sexual desire, arranged the murder of the man whose wife David had seduced, and was eventually called to account for his reprehensible behavior.

Psalm 51 is considered to be his confession of guilt and his prayer for forgiveness. It is one of the few psalms to carry a specific introduction describing its origin:

> To the choirmaster. A Psalm of David,
> when Nathan the prophet came to him,
> after he had gone in to Bathsheba.

In this introduction, David's sin is revealed before all who read the psalm. Just as the name of Pontius Pilate is indelibly associated with the death of Jesus by way of the Christian creeds, so is David's sin uncovered and recounted for all time through this profound and beautiful psalm.

The psalm tells part of the story of a great man's greatest failure. Perhaps for that reason it can bring us solace in our own errant moments. There is comfort in knowing that even the mightiest fall and are held accountable. There is comfort, too, in finding in their experiences words that suit our own lives.

In our adulteries, deceits, abuses, and failures, we can identify with this fallen king. In David's story we can see our own tale told. The words of his heart give shape to the cries of sorrow and shame that pierce our own existence. Through his pleas we can express not only our remorse but also our hopes for healing.

Cleansing

Before we delve further into the incredible hope that follows from this psalm, we can use it to review the most common experiences of a soul on the way to deliverance.

There is in its opening words that familiar appeal to love as the grounds for our deliverance. We rest our hope in a mercy and grace far greater than any individual heart can hold.

Recognizing our own limitations, we look for a source large enough not only to overcome but to completely blot out our faults and failures.

> According to thy abundant mercy
> blot out my transgressions. . . .
> Hide thy face from my sins,
> and blot out all my iniquities.
>
> Psalm 51:1b, 9

In our sorrow and shame we yearn for the obliteration of that which has troubled our life. We reach a point where we simply want it to be over. We want to be free again.

In the same way we long and plead to be made clean, to be restored to a state of purity that will satisfy the primal longing for innocence deep inside us.

> Wash me thoroughly from my iniquity,
> and cleanse me from my sin! . . .
> Purge me with hyssop, and I shall be clean;
> wash me, and I shall be whiter than snow. . . .
> Create in me a clean heart, O God.
>
> Psalm 51:2, 7, 10a

We have known too well how stained life can be. We have sensed our own mortality, our imperfections, and our propensity to make self-serving choices with all the destructive consequences they can bring. That is what the psalmist recognized, too:

> Behold, I was brought forth in iniquity,
> and in sin did my mother conceive me.
>
> Psalm 51:5

With these words the author does not condemn sex or procreation, as some have erroneously argued. Rather, these words express the psalmist's coming to terms with human nature itself—with the fact that we are all imperfect, incapable of living without failure or fault. We are a flawed species still on the way toward perfection. To say this is not to denigrate humanity. It is simply to acknowledge our limits.

In this knowledge, we look beyond ourselves to find our way out of the morass of human brokenness. We come to a point where we are willing to admit we are lost, where we finally will trust a greater wisdom. We relinquish ourselves into the hands of One who is able to wash, purge, and recreate us. We, like the psalmist, open ourselves to being the objects of such active intervention in the hope that once recreated, we, too, can be filled with joy.

Sometimes, as the psalm suggests, this process of cleansing and growth necessitates some kind of purge in our lives. That which obstructs our progress, such as unhealthy patterns from the past, may need to be removed through a kind of psychological or spiritual surgery. Such chastening and discipline of the spirit can be a very painful process. But without it we may not be able to change as much as we need to.

Again, human and divine measures of our progress may differ. The eyes of God may see us as clean long before our peers do or the human institutions that hold sway over our lives. That in itself is testimony to the same kind of imperfection in others from which we ourselves seek release. Those around us and the institutional systems we create also need continual purging and cleansing.

Confession

Perhaps the first step toward cleansing comes through a confrontation with the truth within.

> For I know my transgressions,
>   and my sin is ever before me.
> Against thee, thee only, have I sinned,
>   and done that which is evil in thy sight,
> so that thou art justified in thy sentence.
>
> Psalm 51:3, 4a

Sometimes what we know about ourselves is depressing. It overwhelms and consumes us; it nags and disturbs. We can't seem to be rid of it. Unless we find a way to let it go, it spreads like a plague throughout our life, slowly poisoning our soul, our work, and our relationships. There are things we know about ourselves that we fear others ever discovering. Out of an instinct for self-preservation we keep them well buried. But these hidden secrets can destroy us. They are chunks of life that float around loose and dangerous, jagged and unresolved. The energy it takes to keep them locked up in some private inner corner can steal the very breath from our soul. How can we deal with these secrets? Where can we let them go?

The psalmist found release in confession before One who could not be seen or touched but whose presence and compassion was nevertheless trusted. Frightening though it was to be exposed before such an awesome Judge, the psalmist had the consolation of knowing that before this Judge, the lies were useless anyway. For nothing could be hidden; all was already known. However, because this Judge was also known as compassionate, slow to anger, and abounding in constant love, to disclose those secrets and burdens of the soul was not self-destructive but redemptive.

This God gave the psalmist some place to go with all the shame and pain of life. It was not spiritual suicide to bare the heart's true nature. To do so was the key to the door of deliverance.

In confessing the secrets of the soul to one who will honor our trust, we can surely find great release. But finding a safe place to do that, believing that we will not be rejected or suffer further for our mistakes and faults—that in itself takes a great leap of faith. We so badly need to take that leap. Otherwise the extra burdens we carry will accumulate until we are smothered.

For the psalmist, God was a safe place to turn, for God would not turn away a penitent heart or a wounded soul.

> The sacrifice acceptable to God is a broken spirit;
>   a broken and contrite heart, O God,
>   thou wilt not despise.
>
> Psalm 51:17

Contrition

In the broken spirit there is truth. The contrite heart is the heart through which we most get in touch with ourselves. To have a broken spirit does not mean that our human will is negated, that our value is lost, or that we are reduced to cowering servitude. Rather, it is the point at which we are most purified and refined by the fires of suffering. It is the point at which our truest self often emerges, when we most clearly recognize our vulnerability and the true nature of our relationships with life and those around us.

A side effect of such self-realization is that we can see the wider impact of our decisions and actions. What we thought were private acts carried out in a sphere under our own control may turn out to have ripple effects far beyond our expectations. Thus the psalmist can write, "Against thee, thee only, have I sinned" (Ps 51:4a). God here represents that which seeks our health and well-being, thus it is our own best interests that we ultimately violate. When we come to contrition it is to this understanding that our eyes are opened.

A broken spirit and a contrite heart shatter our false pride. We are unmasked; our disguises and illusions are stripped away. We stare at our naked selves before the roaring cosmos and look up with fragile faces for a power beyond us that can clothe us again, not in the same old, tired fashions but with newer and finer raiments than we have ever known. In the moment of contrition our hearts are finally, fully open. We relinquish our defenses, drop our shields, and bare our souls to a universe in which we hope to find healing.

The psalmist's testimony is that our hope is not in vain. The God Scripture describes is, after all, much more interested in our deliverance than in our destruction. Were that not the case, hope would be life's greatest delusion. For hope, by definition, is a longing for a reality contrary to current conditions.

When the psalmist writes, "thou art justified in thy sentence," it is a recognition that by ordinary standards, there is no point to hope. The logical, fair, and natural consequences of human imperfection entail appropriate judgments and punishments. That is exactly why biblical faith is so extraordinary. Scripture dares to claim that even when our sentences are justified, there is reason to hope. For there is more to life than fate, karma, or the natural consequences of an ordered, mechanistic universe, even one managed by a righteousness-oriented God.

That is not to say that the moral rules of life are suspended for those who fail and then turn in repentance for deliverance. The rules remain, as do most of the consequences. However, Scripture promises that a love exists that is greater than any rules of cause and effect. In this love we can find reason to hope. For this love can accomplish our deliverance—despite the rules—from whatever memories and circumstances oppress us. Though our external circumstances may not immediately change, our hearts and attitudes may be liberated and granted a new vision.

Truth

Part of that vision is a new orientation toward truth.

Behold, thou desirest truth in the inward being;
therefore teach me wisdom in my secret heart.

Psalm 51:6

Behind this petition is a confidence that we are indeed capable of truth. There is faith here in an inner realm of the spirit that is able to perceive and apply wisdom. From examining the truth about ourselves—our failures and longings, weaknesses and gifts, vulnerabilities and possibilities, sufferings and hopes—we gather strength and develop wisdom.

By facing both our true guilt and our real innocence we touch what is most solid in our lives. We discover what it is that we *can* control. By focusing on the immediate inner realities in the context of the greatest possible external framework, we develop an understanding for dealing with life in that intermediate arena, our relationships with others.

In the complex world of truths—and truth always varies with the perspective of the perceiver—we need to find what is true for us, both in the inmost reaches of our soul and in relation to the cosmos as a whole. From there, we can engage more wholistically with the world around us.

Grace

The dominant truth for all of us and behind life itself, claims the psalmist, is a love powerful enough to change our lives and to make us continually new. It is a love that can finally fulfill our deep hunger for joy.

> Fill me with joy and gladness;
>> let the bones which thou hast broken rejoice.
>>>> Psalm 51:8

This healing and joy comes from the partnership described as living in the presence of the One who loves us.

> Cast me not away from thy presence,
>> and take not thy holy Spirit from me.
>>>> Psalm 51:11

It is a joy that produces, as we have seen in other psalms, a desire to respond to our deliverance with praise, testimony, and service within the community of all those who have already known or who yet wait for deliverance.

> Then I will teach transgressors thy ways,
>> and sinners will return to thee. . . .
> O Lord, open thou my lips,
>> and my mouth shall show forth thy praise.
>>>> Psalm 51:13, 15

David

David the king eventually returned to a condition of joy. After great suffering, he was again able to praise God as fully as before. His experience becomes a lesson for others who have failed, suffered, and sought deliverance.

But first, David had to go through a personal hell. When confronted with the searing truth, he summoned the courage to admit it. He publicly confessed and sought forgiveness. Without bitterness or loss of faith, he accepted the consequences of his fall. He implored God to have mercy on those who suffered innocently as a result of his wrongdoing. Yet it remains a heart-rending part of David's story that his first prayers went unanswered. Innocent people did suffer and die. The consequences of that whole tragedy were inexorably played out to their sorrowful conclusion.

It is true that David did not engage in this process alone. There were partners in the deceit, other players in the tragedy, not least of all Bathsheba. Whether she valiantly resisted David's advances, simply acquiesced, or actually encouraged David's desire, we have not a clue. The story is of David's blame, not hers, and of David's confession and remorse. We do not know how Bathsheba felt, how she might have suffered and grieved, or how she dealt with her guilt and pain.

For both of them the penalty was steep. For David, as king of Israel, a public figure and hero, God's chosen and favored servant, the disgrace was enormous. He faced a horrible judgment, both publicly and personally. Those he loved suffered. The people he served suffered. His future and career were indelibly stained.

But that is not the end of David's story. Two sets of consequences were played out after the tragic fall of this great king.

Redemption

There were the consequences of destruction: a child lost, a kingdom damaged, a family in discord. But weaving through the tragedy was also a powerful new thread of life. Out of the betrayal rose an edifice of great grandeur. In the desert of David and Bathsheba's life bloomed a most glorious new flower. The same deliverer who called them to account and required of them a painful chastening brought into their lives a new experience of hope through the birth of a son, Solomon. Scripture says that God loved this child in a very special way. God even gave him a favored name, Jedidiah, which means "beloved of the Lord" (2 Sam 12:24-26).

It is remarkable that of all David's children, the one who was to succeed and surpass him as king was a child born of his love for Bathsheba. Of all the women who were available to mother Israel's next king, who, indeed, had prior claim to the throne, it was Bathsheba whose child was chosen by grace. The offspring of tragedy became the child of promise. Into great grief came astounding consolation. Out of love broken came love renewed.

Nor were David and Bathsheba forever impugned. The same David whose name is displayed in his brokenness in Psalm 51 is the David whose name has continued to signify greatness and promise ever since. His was even the name taken to describe the one considered to be the greatest deliverer of all: Jesus, Son of David.

Bathsheba, too, is associated directly with the birth of the promised Messiah, albeit by virtue of her first marriage and David's violation of it. She is one of only five women mentioned in the geneology of Jesus according to the Gospel of Matthew (Matt 1:1-17).

That geneology is one of the greatest testimonies to grace in all of Scripture, including not only women, but women who might be seen (along with many of the men in the list) as highly unlikely candidates for the Messiah's ancestry: Tamar, so unjustly treated by the man she eventually had to seduce in order to achieve her due (Gen 38); Rahab, the honored prostitute (Josh 6:17, 25); faithful Ruth, the half-breed outcaste (Ruth); Bathsheba, adulteress yet mother of a king (2 Sam: 11–12); and Mary, the poor peasant girl (Luke 1:26-56).

Is it an accident that Scripture so specifically includes these special women in its testimony to the workings of Divine Providence? Is this not a profound parable of grace and the capacity of love to accept, to redeem, and to use fallible people such as ourselves in the most magnificent ways?

Such grace is the very heartbeat of Scripture. It is the pulse of the Divine. In these stories and throughout the psalms we see the power of a love that is available to us, not only to lift us out of whatever pits we may sink into but to utterly transform and renew our lives.

With such powerful love on our side, the future is incredibly open. There are possibilities awaiting us that have yet to be born in our minds. There is no Pit from which our soul cannot be delivered, no darkness that cannot be penetrated by the light of redemption, no wound that cannot be healed.

Affliction will come in life. Adversaries will rise against us. Often will we be our own worst enemies. But beyond all the struggles are endless possibilities for deliverance, based in a love far greater than we can imagine. This is a love that can lead us to truth. It can yield new opportunities for gratitude, for joy, and for service. It can restore us to life in communities where we can find nourishment and support for the days ahead.

What so many psalms tell us is that the days of the Pit can pass. Deliverance can be ours. The same power that brought promise out of tragedy for David and Bathsheba can give birth to newness in our lives as well. Like their child Solomon, we too may become children of the promise, "beloved of the Lord." We, too, like David and Bathsheba, can find beyond our fall both deliverance and a new kind of joy. For there is ultimately no limit to the redemptive possibilities of that almighty love that waits to embrace us all.

> Bless the LORD, O my soul;
>   and all that is within me bless his holy name!
> Bless the LORD, O my soul,
>   and forget not all his benefits,
> who forgives all your iniquity,
>   who heals all your diseases,
> who redeems your life from the Pit,
>   who crowns you with steadfast love and mercy,
> who satisfies you with good as long as you live
>   so that your youth is renewed like the eagle's. . . .
> For as the heavens are high above the earth,
>   so great is his steadfast love toward those who fear
>   him;
> as far as the east is from the west,
>   so far does he remove our transgressions
>   from us. . . .
> Bless the LORD, O my soul!

> Psalm 103:1-5, 11-12, 22b